The Illustrated Word Processing Dictionary

by

RUSSELL A. STULTZ

Prentice-Hall, Inc., Englewood Cliffs, New Jersey 07632

Library of Congress Cataloging in Publication Data

Stultz, Russell Allen
The illustrated word processing dictionary.

Includes index.
1. Word processing (Office practice)—Dictionaries. 2. Word processing (Office practice)—Handbooks, manuals, etc. I. Title.
HF5548.115.S77 651.8 82-5318
ISBN 0-13-450726-6 AACR2
ISBN 0-13-450718-5 (pbk.)

Editorial/production supervision and interior design: ***Joan Foley***
Page layout: ***Margaret Mary Finnerty***
Cover design: ***Diane Saxe***
Manufacturing buyer: ***Ed O'Dougherty***

Printed in the United States of America

10 9 8 7 6 5 4 3 2 1

ISBN 0-13-450726-6 {C}
ISBN 0-13-450718-5 {PBK.}

Prentice-Hall International, Inc., *London*
Prentice-Hall of Australia Pty. Limited, *Sydney*
Prentice-Hall Canada Inc., *Toronto*
Prentice-Hall of India Private Limited, *New Delhi*
Prentice-Hall of Japan, Inc., *Tokyo*
Prentice-Hall of Southeast Asia Pte. Ltd., *Singapore*
Whitehall Books Limited, *Wellington, New Zealand*

CONTENTS

PREFACE

Today, word processing is one of the fastest-growing office technology industries in existence. There are well over one hundred manufacturers of word processing systems, and the diversity of equipment and features is staggering. Although there is a common base of equipment and features, no two systems are the same. Some have unique word processing features and use unique terms to describe them.

With every new word processing system installation comes the need for trained word processing operators. However, it is becoming increasingly difficult to prepare word processing operators for the onslaught of systems and functions. Although there is some knowledge transfer from one system to another, many courses teach rote rather than logic. A basis for understanding is often lacking.

This book is designed to provide the student with a good foundation in word processing systems and functions. It provides a basis for understanding the intent of word processing functions and applications and it contains illustrations of the described functions in action.

Once the word processing student has completed this book, his or her background should be sufficiently broad to allow rapid adaptation to the idiosyncrasies of almost any system on the market.

ABOUT THE AUTHOR

Russell Allen Stultz has been involved in the electronic communications, computer, information and word processing, and educational and publishing industries for more than 24 years. He has written numerous manuals and books covering a wide range of electronic technology topics. In recent years he has conducted international research, written, and lectured on management and productivity.

Included in his works is *The Word Processing Handbook*, a book directed at managers, which is one of the most popular word processing books on the market today. *The Illustrated Word Processing Dictionary*, which is directed at the operator, promises to be of equal importance.

Module 1
INTRODUCTION

PURPOSE OF THIS BOOK

This book is designed for the student of word processing systems, the word processing operator, and the classroom instructor of word processing systems. The student will find descriptions and examples of word processing equipment and standard and advanced word processing features. The fully qualified word processing operator will find convenient reference material and explanations of advanced features that may help in advising management on system selection. The instructor will find a gold mine of examples, explanations, and quizzes that can be used in teaching word processing in the classroom.

Word processing system equipment and functions are described in plain, everyday English. Even the most inexperienced word processing operator will quickly grasp what functions do and typical uses and will enjoy the logical, easy-to-understand, illustrated examples.

HOW TO USE THIS BOOK

To help you progress through this book in a logical manner, you should understand how the book is organized and how information can be located quickly. The book is divided into modules. The first six modules include the introduction and descriptions of word processing system equipment. Module 7 discusses word processing system turn-on and turn-off procedures. Modules 8 through 61 include word processing function descriptions, beginning with the simplest and working up to the more complex. Modules 8 through 61 are organized to introduce each word processing function with a *Description* paragraph, which tells what each function does and explains how it is typically made to work. Next, an *Applications* paragraph discusses the uses or benefits of the word processing function being described.

Finally, a *Typical Operation* paragraph provides a step-by-step procedure and accompanying illustrations to demonstrate how each function is actually performed. Although key sequences vary from system to system, the typical operation paragraph familiarizes the reader with function dynamics. Most of the procedures contained in this book either work on existing display-based word processing systems or are a compromise between the way two or more existing systems operate.

SYMBOLS USED IN ILLUSTRATIONS

Standard symbols are used in the illustrations to show text movement and "highlighting," which sets certain portions of displayed text apart from the rest. You should become familiar with these symbols before studying Modules 8 through 61. The symbols are shown and defined in Table 1.

Table 1 Symbols Used in Illustrations

Symbol	*Meaning*
↑ ⟶ ⤸	Indicates movement
■	Present cursor position
□	Previous cursor position
□⟶■	Indicates cursor movement (previous to present position)
[highlighted bar]	Highlighted text
[lines] OR [lines]	Lines of text
[word blocks]	Lines of text showing words and spaces
L15	Display screen line number

Table 1 Symbols Used in Illustrations (Continued)

Symbol		*Meaning*	
HELLO (caption balloon)		Descriptive captions	
O—M—T—T—A—M (5) (10) (25)(35) (60) (75)		Format line with margins (M), tabs (T), align tabs (A), and outline tab (O). Character positions shown by numbers in parentheses.	
	Screen Graphic Symbols		
◀	Return	>	Indent
▶	Standard Tab	●	Period
▲	Align Tab	{s}	Imbedded Code
◆	Center	o	Space

TERMS AND DEFINITIONS

Some word processing terms used in this book are defined in Table 2. The word processing functions that are the subject of entire modules are defined in the first paragraph of their respective module; therefore, these terms are not repeated in Table 2.

Table 2 Terms and Definitions

Term	*Definition*
Character	A letter, number, punctuation mark, space, or symbol displayed on a screen or printed on paper.
Character position	A specific position on the display screen, such as the intersection of display screen line 3, character position 45.
Character string	Any unique sequence of characters.
Close document	The act of filing a displayed document on the word processing system storage medium.
Cursor	A flashing square or underscore that shows the display screen position at which a typed character will appear.
Escape	A key sequence that either completes or cancels a word processing function.
Execute	The key sequence, which includes pressing one or two special keys, to complete the execution of a word processing function.

Table 2 Terms and Definitions (Continued)

Term	*Definition*
Imbedded code	A special key sequence typed within text which performs some special function, such as stopping the printer (Stop Code).
Key sequence	Any key stroke or combination of key strokes that serves as an instruction to a word processing system.
Open document	The act of displaying a stored document on the word processing system display screen.
Protocols	A telecommunications code that complies with an established pattern, or specification.
Storage medium	A magnetic storage device, such as a disk, tape, or card, used to file documents electronically.
Supershift	An extra keyboard shift, activated by a special key sequence, that allows standard character keys to type a third character, where lowercase and uppercase are the first two.
Text	Words, sentences, paragraphs, or financial information used to make up the body of a document.
Type face	The specific type style, such as gothic or italic.
Type font	The mechanical device, such as a daisy wheel or Selectric ball, containing the type characters.

Module 2

DISPLAY-BASED WORD PROCESSING SYSTEM CATEGORIES

DESCRIPTION

This book deals with half-page and full-page display-based word processing systems. These systems use display screens to create and edit (or change) documents.

There are several advantages to display-based word processing systems. First, a document can be typed, reviewed, and changed on a display screen before printing it on paper. As changes are being made, manipulation of characters and words can be viewed on the screen, ensuring that the proper results will be achieved.

There are non-display-based word processors that require that paper be used to visualize changes. There are also display-based word processing systems that use single-line strip displays. These are not specifically discussed or illustrated in this book, although many of the functions described are available on these systems.

The three general categories of display-based word processing systems are

1. Stand-alone systems
2. Shared-logic systems
3. Distributed-logic systems

This module briefly describes each category.

STAND-ALONE SYSTEMS

Figure 1 contains a diagram of a stand-alone word processing system. Stand-alone word processing systems are self-contained, single operator units. They can be compared to an office typewriter, which is a stand-alone word processor of the simplest type. Stand-alone word processors have a typewriter keyboard and display screen (called a work station), a printing device, central processing unit (CPU) components including an electronic memory, and a storage device. The central processing unit and memory in combination with system software (programmed word processing instructions) give the system its electronic "intelligence" to perform word processing functions in response to operator keystrokes.

The storage device is used to save, or file, electronically created documents. The documents can be recalled from the storage device for editing, printing, or copying to secondary storage devices. Storage devices and media, as well as keyboards, displays, and printer devices, are all described in the following modules.

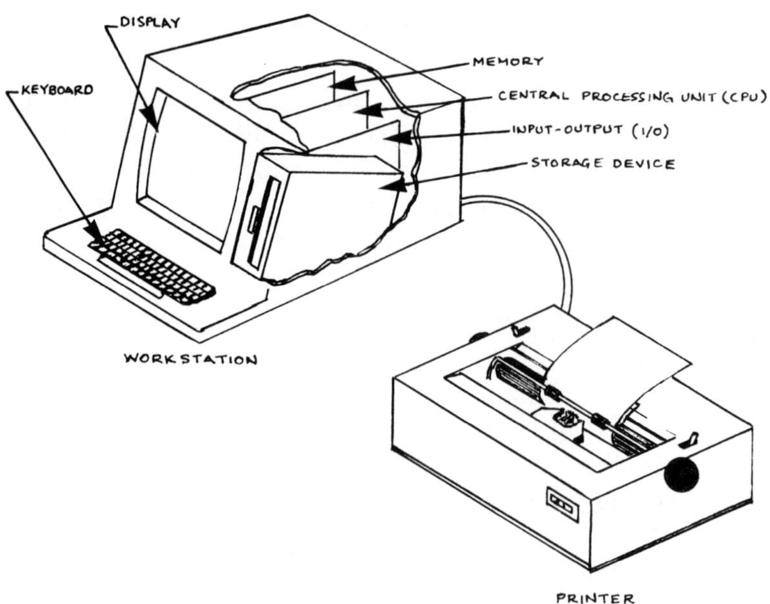

Figure 1 A Stand-Alone Word Processing System

SHARED-LOGIC SYSTEMS

Figure 2 contains a diagram of a shared-logic system. This system configuration shares system resources including the CPU, the printer, and sometimes the system storage device. Shared-logic systems support two or more work stations, thereby allowing two or more word processing operators to use the system simultaneously. Shared-logic systems often become "sluggish" as the operator load increases. Two or more operators can cause the CPU to be interrupted, slowing its response to individual operators. Another drawback of shared-logic systems is that the entire system can be rendered inoperable if one of the shared resources malfunctions.

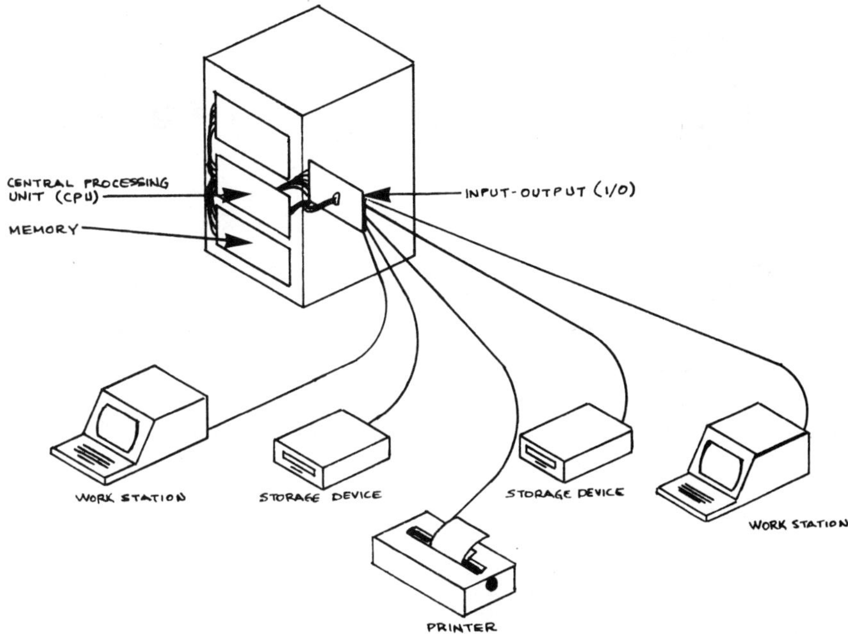

Figure 2 A Shared-Logic Word Processing System

DISTRIBUTED-LOGIC SYSTEMS

Figure 3 contains a diagram of a distributed-logic system. This system configuration places limited intelligence in each work station, which makes system response time virtually immune to operator loading. The shared-logic system also shares system resources. However, those systems that have individual storage devices located with each work station are less susceptible to total system failure when one system component malfunctions. If the system's CPU fails, the total system will of course be inoperable just as in the case of the shared-logic system.

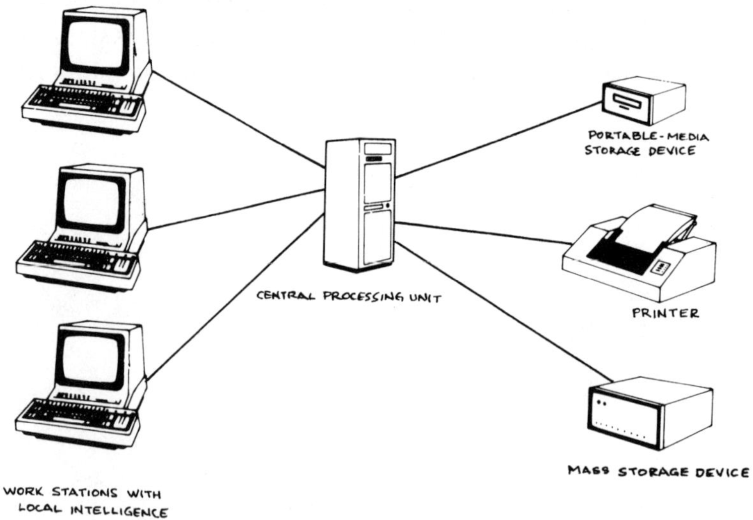

Figure 3 A Distributed-Logic Word Processing System

Module 3

WORD PROCESSING SYSTEM WORK STATIONS

DESCRIPTION

Word processing system work stations include the display screen and the typewriter keyboard. Some work stations also include the system's storage device, such as a magnetic tape or disk drive, used to record documents for future use. This module describes work station display screens and keyboards.

DISPLAY SCREENS

Word processing display screens are of three general types:

1. Partial-page display screens
2. Full-page display screens
3. Two-page display screens

Partial-Page Display Screens As the term implies, a partial-page display screen shows only a part of a page. The majority of word processing screens display an eighty-character line width, although some displays are wider. The number of lines vary from around twelve to twenty-five. A full page of text, which may be around fifty-seven lines of text, cannot be viewed in its entirety on a partial-page display screen. To see an entire page on a twenty-two-line partial-page display screen, it must be viewed in three twenty-two-line sections.

The entire display area is called a "screen load." A twenty-two-line by eighty-character-wide display, then, has a screen load of 1,760 characters (22 times 80).

Some systems have a "zoom" feature which allows the entire page to be displayed in miniature. In other words, a miniature page can be viewed to check page layout, including margin and paragraph appearance. However, since the text is reduced in size, it is difficult to read.

Full-Page Display Screens A full-page display screen shows an entire page of text, equivalent to an 8½-by-11-inch sheet of paper. Although many full-page display screens are only eighty characters wide, they usually show up to sixty lines of text at a time. This allows the operator to see the page layout as it is being typed.

Two-Page Display Screens Two-page display screens show two pages at a time, positioned side by side on the screen. Usually, the displayed pages are sequential, so that adjoining text can be checked. However, two-page display screens are not restricted to displaying adjoining pages. If, for example, text will be transferred from one page to another, the operator may wish to display the source page and the destination page.

Other Display Screen Features Display screens often feature antireflection filters, which are screens or tinted panels that cut down reflected light. Some are built to tilt so that they can be adjusted to minimize uncomfortable light reflections.

WORD PROCESSING SYSTEM KEYBOARDS

Word processing system keyboards incorporate a standard typewriter keyboard including lowercase and uppercase letters, numbers, punctuation marks, and common typewriter symbols such as the dollar sign, percentage sign, and asterisk. The keyboard also includes the RETURN, TAB, BACKSPACE, and SHIFT keys. In addition to the standard typewriter keys, special word processing function keys are included. The keys vary from system to system, depending on the approach used to perform word processing functions.

There are three general types of word processing keyboards:

1. Code-key keyboards
2. Mnemonic keyboards

3. Combination code-key, mnemonic keyboards

Code-Key Keyboards The code-key keyboard has individual function keys, which, when pressed, instruct the word processing system to perform some special word processing system function. These keyboards normally have more keys than others, in that a special key exists for most word processing system commands. For example, the INSERT code key is pressed to insert new text within existing text.

Mnemonic Keyboards Differing from the code-key keyboard, mnemonic keyboards have very few special keys. These word processing keys are normally used in combination with standard character keys to perform word processing functions. For example, the key sequence for INSERT might be to press a key labeled CONTROL in combination with the "I" key. Mnemonic keyboard systems are usually designed so that the keys used in the sequence can easily be remembered. The insert function key sequence might be CONTROL I, delete might be CONTROL D, printer stop might be CONTROL S, and so forth.

Combination Code-Key, Mnemonic Keyboards These keyboards are a compromise between the code-key and mnemonic keyboard systems. They use code keys to perform frequently used functions, such as INSERT and DELETE, and they use a special CONTROL key in combination with character keys to perform less frequently used word processing functions.

Module 4

COMMON WORD PROCESSING SYSTEM PRINTING DEVICES

DESCRIPTION

A number of printing devices are used in conjunction with word processing systems. Most are of "letter quality," that is, the printed output is suitable for office correspondence. In fact, a document prepared on a letter quality printer looks exactly as if it had been typed on a standard electric office typewriter. Devices that are considered letter quality include

1. Daisy wheel printers
2. Thimble printers
3. Selectric (spherical font) printers
4. Intelligent office copiers
5. Ink jet printers
6. Laser printers

Non-letter-quality printers are also used on word processing systems. These include

1. Matrix printers
2. Line printers

These printers were adopted from data processing systems. Although the type quality is not considered letter quality, these printers are faster and often more reliable than conventional letter quality printers.

The printers listed above fall into impact and nonimpact printer categories. A brief description of impact and nonimpact printers is provided in the following paragraphs of this module.

IMPACT PRINTERS

Impact printers use mechanical type fonts. These fonts are positioned so that the selected character can strike a typewriter ribbon, leaving the character impression on paper. Daisy wheel, thimble, Selectric, matrix, and line printers are all in the impact printer family.

Daisy Wheel Printers Daisy wheel printers are the most commonly used type in word processing. These printers resemble a typewriter without a keyboard. A carrier advances the type font and ribbon horizontally across the paper. The paper, which rests against a standard typewriter platen, is advanced vertically by platen rotation, just as on a standard typewriter.

The daisy wheel resembles a daisy flower with thin radiating petals. Each petal contains a letter, number, or symbol at the end. The daisy wheel rotates to the selected character position, and a plunger strikes the character petal, leaving an image on the paper.

Some daisy wheel printers, called twin track or dual head, have two print carriers. Each contains a ribbon and a daisy wheel of its own. Dual-head printers allow both standard and special characters and symbols, such as Greek or math, to be printed in combination without having to change the type font each time an alternate type style is needed.

Thimble Printers The major difference between thimble printers and daisy wheel printers is the type-font configuration. Thimble printers use a type font that resembles a thimble, or vertically oriented cylinder. The type characters are arranged in rows and columns around the circumference of the thimble. The thimble is rotated and elevated so that the selected character position strikes the printer's ribbon against the paper, leaving an impression.

Selectric Printers The Selectric Typewriter, manufactured by IBM, uses a spherical font resembling a ball. Like the thimble font, type characters are arranged in rows and columns around the circumference of the sphere. The sphere is rotated so that the selected character position strikes the printer's ribbon against the paper, leaving an impression.

Matrix Printers Matrix printers, which are not considered letter quality, use vertical columns and horizontal rows of print pins, which impact the printer ribbon in combinations that form letters. For example, the capital letter I is formed by a centered vertical column of pins. The plus sign is formed by a centered vertical column and horizontal row of pins.

Line Printers Line printers are among the fastest impact printers. Line printers print entire lines of characters at a time. A common type of line printer uses vertical strings, or "chains," of characters which correspond to each character position on a horizontal line of text. For example, if the line printer produces a 150-character line, there would be 150-character chains. The chains are positioned simultaneously to represent all the characters to be printed on a line. Once positioned, the entire row of chains strikes the printer's ribbon against the paper, leaving the line of text.

NONIMPACT PRINTERS

Three nonimpact printers are described in the following paragraphs: the ink jet printer, the laser printer, and the intelligent image copier.

Ink Jet Printers Ink jet printers spray droplets of liquid ink configured into character shapes on paper. Ink jet printers are faster than daisy printers. These printers are equipped with special envelope-handling mechanisms, which makes them ideal for an operation specializing in form letters.

Laser Printers Laser printers are also high-speed devices. The laser printer uses a beam of high-intensity light to heat character images on a cylinder. The hot image picks up black toner and offsets it on paper, thus reproducing the character image. Laser printers can produce a variety of type styles and sizes and are noted for their good quality.

Intelligent Image Copiers Intelligent image copiers are much like standard office copiers. Instead of scanning an original page of typed text, the intelligent image copier creates a page from word processing system-created data. Documents that have been created on word processing systems and stored in the form of electronic data can be communicated to an intelligent image copier. The copier reproduces the page on a cylinder and offsets it on paper. Like the laser printer, intelligent image copiers often feature several different type styles.

Module 5
PAPER FEED DEVICES

DESCRIPTION

Paper feed devices, including continuous-form paper feeders (or forms tractors), and sheet feeders are used to save paper-handling time on word processing systems. Both of these devices are described in this module.

FORMS TRACTORS

Forms tractors are used to advance continuous-form paper through a word processing printer. Most daisy wheel and thimble printers are equipped to use forms tractors, which can be installed or removed in a matter of seconds. This allows either continuous-form or single-sheet paper to be used on word processing printers. Forms tractors are generally an integral part of matrix and line printers, which are often restricted to the use of continuous-form paper.

To save having to feed a single sheet of paper at a time for multiple-page documents, word processing operators often use continuous-form paper, which has pin feed holes at the outside edges. Forms tractors have feed pins, on either a continuous belt or a sprocket, which fit through the holes to advance the paper a line at a time. In addition to vertically feeding continuous-form paper, forms tractors maintain paper alignment, ensuring straight margins and even lines of text on each page.

SHEET FEEDERS

Sheet feeders are devices built to feed single sheets of paper into word processing printers. Cut sheets, which are most often standard 8½-by-11-inch pieces of paper, are stacked in sheet feeders. As each new sheet of paper is needed, the feeder automatically inserts a new sheet in the printer, thus saving the word processing operator the time necessary to manually feed a sheet of paper for each page to be printed. Twin sheet feeders are also available. These allow selection between two types of paper. For example, the first page of a document may be printed on letterhead; the second and subsequent sheets may be printed on plain bond paper.

ENVELOPE HANDLERS

Envelope handlers are used to feed envelopes into the word processing system printer. These devices are of particular value in operations specializing in direct-mail advertising or customer response. The envelopes are stacked in a tray and fed into the printer one at a time. Like the cut sheet feeders, the envelope handler can be a time saving tool to the word processing operator.

Module 6
STORAGE DEVICES AND MEDIA

DESCRIPTION

Word processing systems use several different types of storage devices and corresponding storage media. The most frequently used today include

1. Eight-inch floppy diskettes
2. Five and ¼-inch mini diskettes
3. Hard disks of various sizes
4. Magnetic tapes
5. Magnetic cards

All of these are magnetic media that allow characters to be electronically stored and recalled. Diskettes and disks are flat platters that resemble phonograph records. Diskettes are portable and can be stored in file cabinets or easily carried from one location to another. Magnetic tapes, which are encased in large reels or cassettes, and cards, which are the size of a standard computer punch card, can also be stored in file cabinets or easily carried from one location to another.

Some hard disks are removable and transportable, although these are several times larger than either the five- or eight-inch floppy diskettes. Most hard disks, however, are contained in a cabinet and must be installed and removed by a qualified service representative. As might be expected, large storage devices usually have more file space than do the small storage devices.

STORAGE CAPACITIES

The type, size, and density of the magnetic media used govern the amount of text that can be stored. Hard disks and large tape can store thousands of pages of text at a time. Five- and eight-inch diskettes can store from fifty to slightly over one hundred pages, depending on the particular system being used and the average number of characters stored on each page.

Diskette densities also influence storage capacity. Some eight-inch diskettes, for example, are single-sided, single-density. Others are double-sided, double-density. This means that one density diskette can store two to four times more information than another of the same physical size.

DOCUMENT ACCESS SPEED

The time it takes for a word processing system to search for, find, and retrieve a stored document depends on the type of storage medium used. Finding a document stored on magnetic tape requires that the tape be transported (wound) until the tape read head recognizes the address (identifying characters) of the filed document. The physical tape travel required to search out a document address can take from a few seconds to minutes.

Search time is greatly reduced when locating a document on a disk-type storage medium. The disk rotates and the magnetic read head travels across the surface of the disk. Finding a document address rarely takes more than a few seconds.

HANDLING MAGNETIC STORAGE MEDIA

Documents that are magnetically stored are vulnerable to loss from magnetic fields produced by metal objects, electric motors, or magnets. A disk can also be physically damaged by abrasions, punctures, bending, and temperature extremes. This means that diskettes must be carefully stored in a cool, dry place away from magnetic fields, in paper jackets, and in special protective storage boxes.

Copy stands that use magnets to hold paper are a common culprit. Inexperienced word processing operators sometimes rest diskettes on magnetic copy stands, resulting in destruction of their stored document.

Another common abuse of magnetic media is writing on a diskette jacket with a ballpoint pen or hard pencil. Bearing down can score the disk and damage its coated surface. Only felt-tip pens should be used to write on diskette jackets, and they should be used lightly.

STORAGE MEDIA SECURITY (BACKUP)

It's a good policy to have backup copies of magnetically created documents. In the event of a system malfunction or diskette damage, the backup copy will serve as insurance. All modern word processing systems allow copies of diskettes to be made for backup. Some word processing systems that use large-capacity hard disks allow the entire disk to be duplicated on a backup disk. Where this cannot be done, copies of individual documents can usually be made on eight-inch diskettes for archival storage.

Backup is always a good policy, and every word processing operation should have a routine backup procedure.

Module 7
TURNING THE EQUIPMENT ON AND OFF

DESCRIPTION

It's extremely important that you read your word processing system's instruction manual carefully before turning the system on or off. First, it should be plugged into a good grade power source. Many word processing system suppliers will not perform system installation without isolated, "computer-grade" power, which is free from voltage fluctuations caused by other equipment plugged into the same circuit.

Once the equipment is plugged into the proper power source, follow the turn-on and turn-off procedures exactly as outlined in your instruction manual. Failure to do so could cause loss of stored documents on the system's storage media.

It is particularly important to insert and remove storage media, such as magnetic diskettes, tapes, or cards, in the proper sequence. Systems often require a special keystroke sequence to be followed when inserting and removing storage media. This too is required to prevent document loss.

Because the turn-on and turn-off procedures are so varied, no attempt is made here to supply a general procedure.

Module 8
CURSOR CONTROL

DESCRIPTION

The cursor (some people like to call it "the pointer") is a flashing or bright dot, square, or underscore character that shows the position on the screen where characters or spaces are being entered. The cursor can be moved both horizontally and vertically. Some systems restrict cursor movement to areas where text has been created, while others allow the cursor to be moved anywhere on the screen.

APPLICATIONS

Most word processors use seven keys for standard cursor movement. These are the four "arrow" keys, referred to as up (North), down (South), left (West), and right (East), the space bar, the BACKSPACE key, and the RETURN key. On some systems some of the cursor control keys are "typomatic" or "repeat," that is, they allow the cursor to advance automatically by holding the key down. Others require a keystroke for each space increment. Three spaces, for example, require three keystrokes.

Character keys are used to enter the corresponding symbols on the screen, which displaces the cursor one place to the right. The TAB key moves the cursor from the left margin to the first tab, or from tab to tab, as set on the format line.

TYPICAL OPERATION

In this illustration the cursor will be moved from the first character of the first line of the displayed document to the twenty-fifth character of the twenty-first line.

1. With the document displayed, note that the cursor is on the first character (the left margin) of the first line.

2. Press the down arrow (South) key until the cursor is on the twenty-first line of the page. (Note that the status line indicates "line 21" or "21,1.")

3. Press the right arrow (East) key until the cursor is on the twenty-fifth character of the twenty-first line. (Note that the status line indicates "character 25" or "21,25.")

Module 9
WORD PROCESSING SYSTEM PROMPTS

DESCRIPTION

Word processing system prompts are messages that are displayed on the screen either to instruct the operator to take some action or to simply inform the operator about the status of the system. Prompts, then, are of two types: action prompts and information prompts. An action prompt may require the operator to insert a diskette, move the cursor to some selected point on the screen, or type some key sequence. An information prompt may simply tell the operator about the status of the system or document being produced. It is there for information only.

Prompts normally appear in a designated area of the display screen, usually at the top or bottom, and are frequently highlighted. That is, they are brighter, are outlined in some way, or flash on and off to attract attention.

To signal the word processing operator to look at prompts, some systems use an audible tone, or "beep," in conjunction with displayed prompts.

APPLICATIONS

Action prompts instruct the operator to do a number of things, including the steps necessary to perform certain system functions. Action prompts may be in the form of statements or questions. For example, if the operator decides to delete, or erase, a sentence, he or she may place the cursor on the first character of text to be deleted and press the DELETE key sequence. The prompt may say

"SELECT TEXT FOR DELETION" or "DELETE WHAT?" In either case, the prompt tells the operator what's required.

An information prompt may tell the operator that the system is busy performing some housekeeping task, and that he or she will have to wait momentarily until the task is completed. For example, once the operator responds to an action prompt "LOAD A SYSTEM DISKETTE," the information prompt "SYSTEM DISKETTE LOADING" may inform the operator that the system is in the process of accepting and storing the word processing system operating software in the system's memory.

TYPICAL OPERATION

In this illustration you are preparing to print a document when a prompt appears which reads, "PRINTER NEEDS PAPER OR RIBBON OR IS OFF LINE."

1. Note prompt "PRINTER NEEDS PAPER OR RIBBON OR IS OFF LINE."

2. Check printer to ensure that paper and ribbon supplies are properly loaded and that the printer power is turned on. (On some systems, you may need to check other items including switch settings and open covers.)

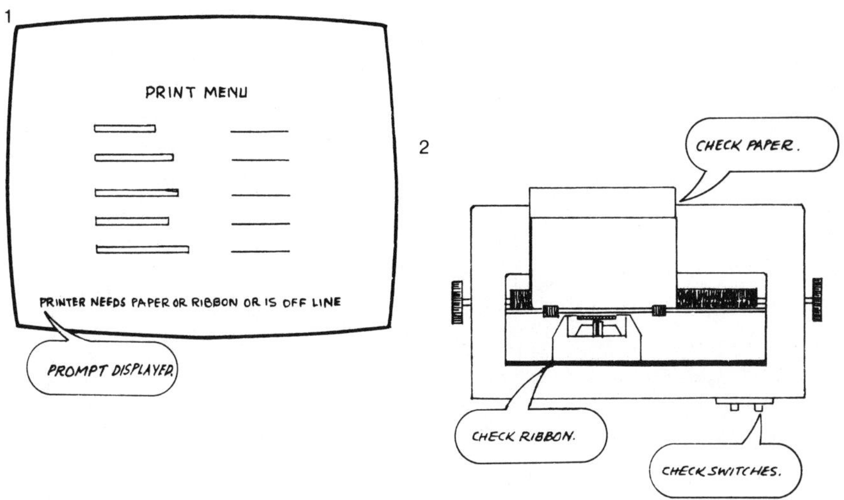

3. Once these are verified, reenter system printing sequence, checking to see that the prompt does not reappear.
4. Print your document.

Module 10
MENUS

DESCRIPTION

Menus are listed on the display screen and offer word processing function selections just as menus in restaurants offer available food selections. In word processing, menus are used to inform the operator of the available selections and to provide guidance. A system with good, easy-to-understand menus can almost be self-teaching.

Selections within menus are made by moving the cursor to the proper line and pressing the system's EXECUTE key sequence or by filling in appropriate spaces within the body of the menu before proceeding to the next step. If you fail to fill in the menu properly, most systems provide appropriate prompts to help you satisfy all menu requirements.

Many menus contain "default" selection values, which are usually the most commonly used values. The existing defaults save operator keyboarding time but may be overridden by simply striking over them with a different value. For example, if the system default is 12-pitch printing, you may change it to "10" by changing the "2" in 12 to a "zero" within the menu.

You may see a menu that offers a variety of selections including "PRINT." The menu may state "PRESS P FOR PRINT." When "P" is pressed, a submenu may appear giving you such printing options as margins, page length, and pitch.

APPLICATIONS

There are two general categories of menus, although some systems don't differentiate between them. These are main menus and submenus. Main menus allow selection of general system functions. Submenus offer a selection of some subset of options available under the general system function. Several of the word processing functions described in this book use menus, and you'll see how several different kinds of menus are used as you progress through the functions.

TYPICAL OPERATION

In this illustration a main menu and submenu will be used to print a document.

> **1.** Select "PRINT DOCUMENT" by moving the cursor to the proper line and pressing the EXECUTE key sequence.
> **2.** Using the resulting print submenu, type in the desired document parameters to print page 2, 10-pitch, justified right-hand margin, on printer number 03. Note that you will have to strike over some of the system submenu defaults.
> **3.** Once the submenu is filled in properly, press the EXECUTE key sequence to begin printing.

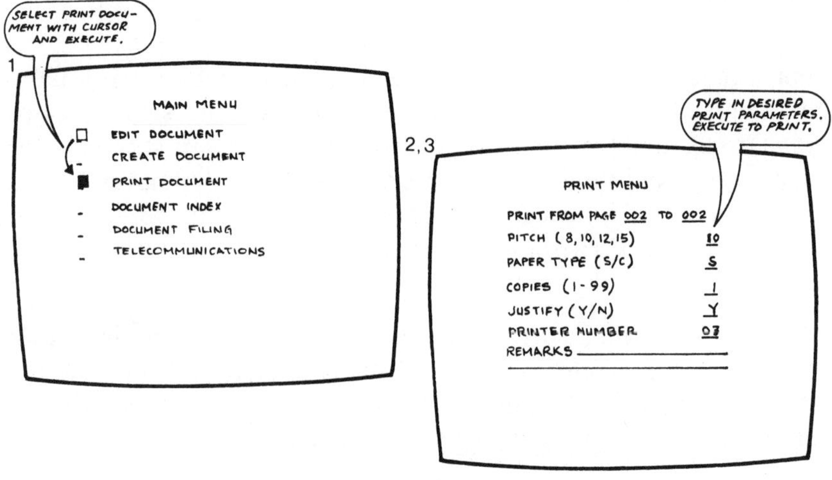

Module 11

DOCUMENT FILING AND RETRIEVAL

DESCRIPTION

Document filing is the process used by a word processing system to save a document for future printing or editing on the system's storage device, such as a magnetic disk, card, or tape. *Document retrieval* is the process used by a word processing system to recall the stored document to the screen for editing, copying, or printing.

The ease of document filing and retrieval is important to the functionality of word processing systems. On almost every system the operator assigns a unique identifying name or number to each document when it is created or before it is filed on the system's storage media. For document retrieval many systems use menus containing a list of document names. These are sometimes combined with appropriate functions, such as "edit," "print," "delete," or "copy," allowing the operator to select a document by pointing to it with the cursor and then performing the desired function by pressing the appropriate key, such as *E, P, D,* or *C.* Other systems let the operator select the function first, including creating a new document, and then identify the document or assign a new name in the case of creating a new one.

APPLICATIONS

The filing and retrieval function on a word processing system is similar to filing and retrieving documents from a file cabinet except that electronic filing and retrieval is much faster.

TYPICAL OPERATION

In this illustration document creation will be selected, and it will be named, typed, stored, and recalled for editing.

1. With the system's main menu displayed, choose "Create Document" with the cursor and press the EXECUTE key sequence.

2. Name the document "MEMO," fill in other menu entries, and proceed to the first blank screen (page 1) by pressing the EXECUTE key sequence.

3. Type the memo (assuming the default format is correct).

4. Press the FILE key sequence and note that the document is stored.

5. Recall the document by moving the cursor to "Edit Document," pressing the EXECUTE key sequence, typing the document name "MEMO" (in some cases the document number would be used), and pressing the EXECUTE key sequence to display the document.

6. Note that the document MEMO is displayed for editing.

TYPE DOCUMENT. USE FILE KEY SEQUENCE TO SAVE.
3,4
LS 1 DOC. MEMO PG 1 CURSOR 1,10
M M

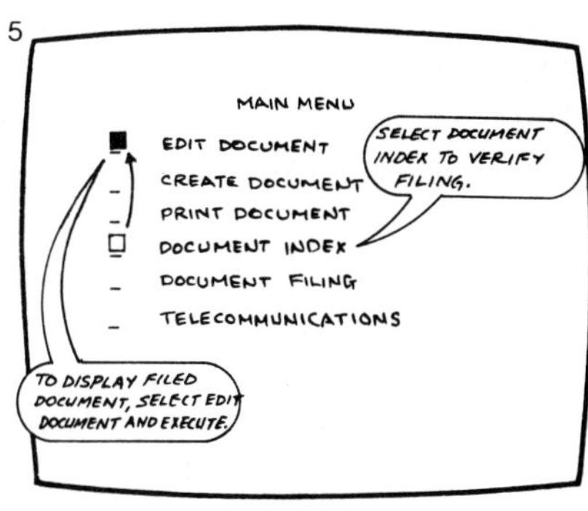
5
MAIN MENU
EDIT DOCUMENT
CREATE DOCUMENT
PRINT DOCUMENT
DOCUMENT INDEX
DOCUMENT FILING
TELECOMMUNICATIONS
SELECT DOCUMENT INDEX TO VERIFY FILING.
TO DISPLAY FILED DOCUMENT, SELECT EDIT DOCUMENT AND EXECUTE.

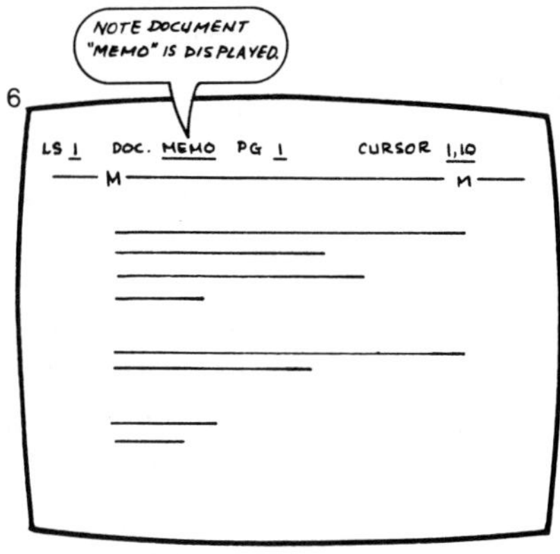
NOTE DOCUMENT "MEMO" IS DISPLAYED.
6
LS 1 DOC. MEMO PG 1 CURSOR 1,10
M M

Module 12
SCREEN GRAPHICS

DESCRIPTION

Screen graphics, which are special symbols displayed on the screens of some word processing systems, are used to indicate where special characters, such as tabs, returns, centers, indents, and even spaces, exist within a document. A few systems allow these screen graphics to be "turned on" or "turned off" in order to see what the text looks like without the special symbols.

APPLICATIONS

Screen graphics allow operators to examine a document to determine exactly what keystrokes were used to create it. For example, Was a line moved over from the left margin with spaces or with a tab? The screen graphics will show this by displaying either one tab symbol or several spaces. How many blank lines exist between two paragraphs? Operators can count the return key symbols to see how many lines were entered. Typical screen graphics are included in Table 1 of this book.

TYPICAL OPERATION

In this illustration screen graphics will be examined to determine how many blank lines exist between the end of the first paragraph and the title of the second paragraph. The method used to indent the first line of each paragraph will also be determined.

1. Determine the blank lines between the end of the first paragraph and the title of the second paragraph by counting the return symbols. Note that there are two.

2. Determine the indention method of the first line of the first paragraph. Note that a tab was used because a tab symbol is shown.

3. Determine the indention method of the first line of the second paragraph. Note that spaces were used because five space symbols are shown.

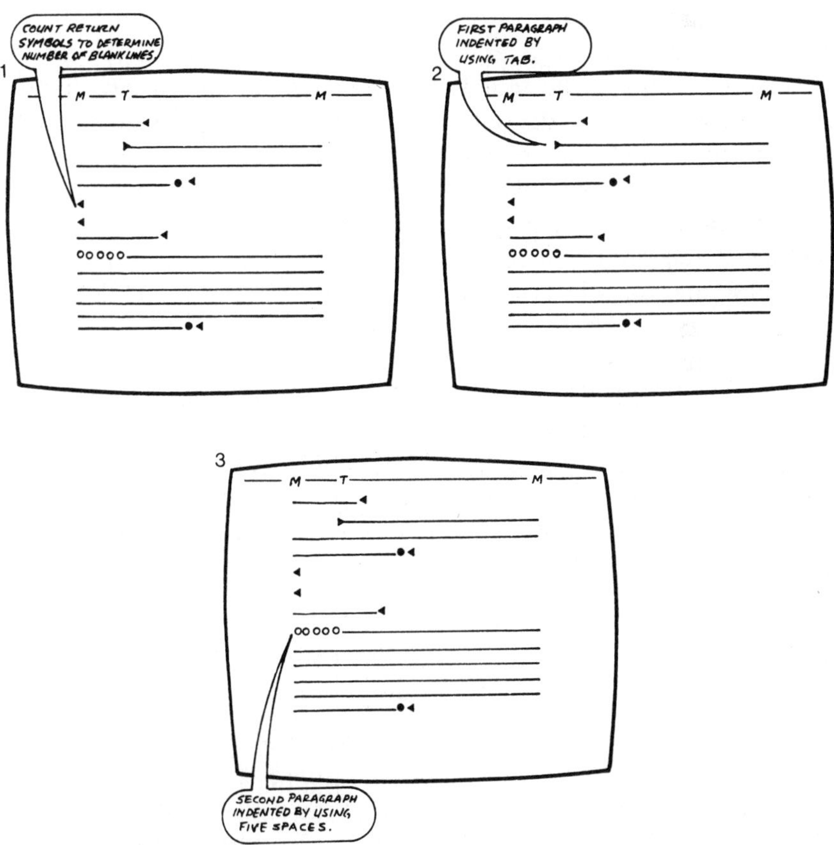

Module 13
RETURN (CARRIAGE RETURN)

DESCRIPTION

The RETURN key, sometimes labeled ENTER or CAR RET (for carrier return), terminates lines of text and adds blank lines. When pressed at the end of a line of text, it moves the cursor to the left-hand margin of the following line. At this point, a new line of text can be typed or the RETURN key can be pressed again to add an additional line space. When text already exists on a page, the return key can be used on some word processing systems just like the down arrow (South) key to move the cursor toward the bottom of the displayed page. The cursor will of course "hug" the left-hand margin when moving it down with the RETURN key.

Some word processing systems have "destructive" RETURN keys where a RETURN graphic symbol is entered each time the RETURN is pressed. When this is the case, the characters beneath the cursor will be replaced by a RETURN symbol each time the RETURN key is pressed. Obviously, you wouldn't want to use the RETURN key for downward cursor movement on systems that use a destructive RETURN.

APPLICATIONS

The RETURN key is used on word processing systems in the same way that it is used on typewriters. The key is used to end lines of text and move to the left-hand margin of the next line. As mentioned above, it is also used to insert blank lines within a document, as between paragraphs.

TYPICAL OPERATION

In this illustration the RETURN key will be used to end the last line of text of a paragraph (ending on line 16), insert a double-line space (lines 17 and 18), and move to the first line of the second paragraph (line 19). We'll assume that the system we're using displays a graphic return symbol.

1. Following the last character (a period) of the first paragraph (located on line 16), press the RETURN key. Note that the RETURN symbol appears and the cursor moves to the left margin of line 17.

2. Press the RETURN key two more times. Note that the RETURN symbols appear on lines 17 and 18 and that the cursor is now located on line 19.

3. Begin typing the first line of the second paragraph (line 19).

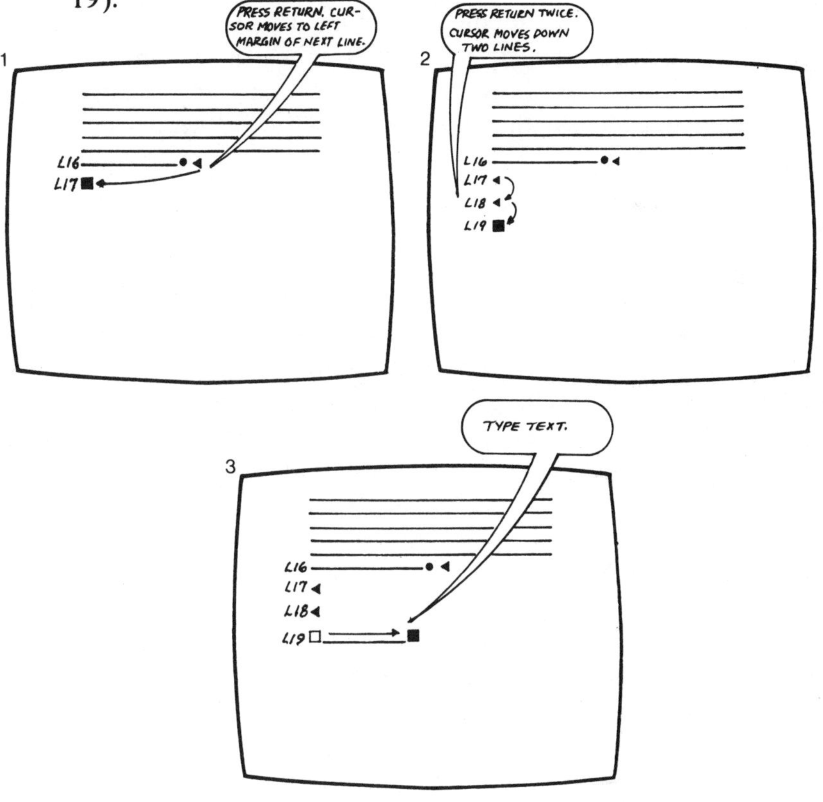

Module 14
AUTOMATIC WORD WRAP

DESCRIPTION

Automatic word wrap is a helpful display-based word processing system function that is used to return the cursor to the beginning of the next line of text automatically when the preceding line reaches the right margin. Text can be typed continuously without using the RETURN key to move to the beginning of the following line of text. Words that begin near the end of a line of text that are too long to fit will be moved, or "wrapped around," to the beginning of the next line, hence the term *automatic word wrap.*

APPLICATIONS

Because the word wrap function automatically shifts the cursor and words that are too long to fit on a line of text to the next line, it is an excellent timesaver. The word processing operator need not be concerned with watching line length or pressing the return key at the end of each line of text. This saves keystrokes and lets the operator concentrate on the text being transcribed.

TYPICAL OPERATION

In this illustration a paragraph of text will be typed by using automatic word wrap. The text will begin on line 3 and end in the middle of line 9.

1. With the cursor at the left margin of the first line of text,

press the RETURN key until it is at the beginning of line 3.

2. Begin typing the paragraph text, disregarding line endings. Note that the cursor and words too long to fit on a line automatically "wrap" to the beginning of the next line.

3. After the last sentence of the paragraph, press the RETURN key. Note that the cursor moves to the left margin of line 10.

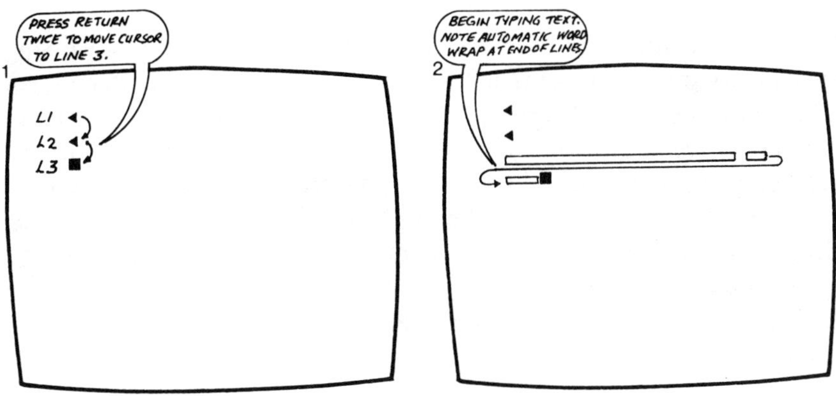

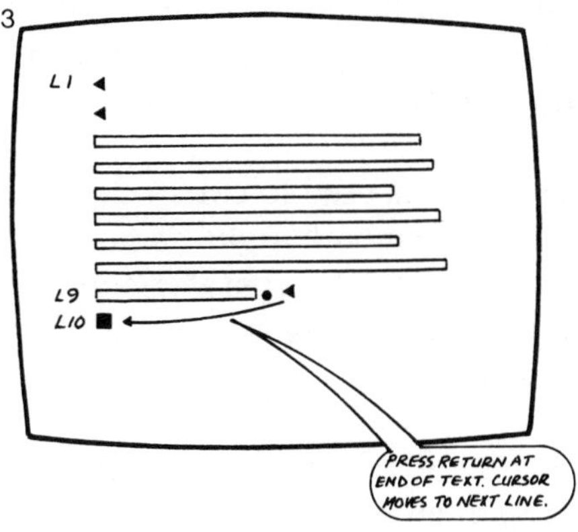

Module 15
SCREEN STATUS LINES

DESCRIPTION

Screen status lines are used on most display-based word processing systems to provide information about the document being displayed. The status line, which appears at the bottom or top of the screen, normally occupies two lines. One line shows document format, including margins and tabs, which is described in detail in the next module of this book. The other line includes such information as document identification (name, number, etc.), page number (on systems capable of multiple-page documents), cursor position (line and character location), and line spacing (single, space and one-half, double, etc.).

The status line is normally set by the operator when a document is created. Often, "default" values that exist within the status line may be those that are most commonly used. However, if the operator determines that values such as margin and tab settings should be changed, they can be readjusted by moving the cursor to the status line through a special key sequence and changing the defaults in the same way that menus are changed.

Sometimes the status line is used to enter other format control codes, such as "justification" (smooth right-hand margin) or "hyphenation." When this is the case, the operator may enter the justification or hyphenation mode by typing a *J* or an *H* in the appropriate location on the status line.

Once the status line is adjusted, the operator returns the cursor to the text area of the screen by pressing the RETURN or EXECUTE key. At this point, the operator may begin keyboarding text and tabular material within the body of the page.

APPLICATIONS

In general, the screen status line is used to tell the operator which document is displayed, which page in the document is displayed, and the exact position of the cursor by line number and character number.

TYPICAL OPERATION

In this illustration the screen status line will be used to determine the document and page displayed and the precise cursor position.

1. With a document displayed, refer to the status line to determine the document. Note that DOC ID 0701A is displayed.

2. Determine which page is displayed. Note that page 6 is displayed.

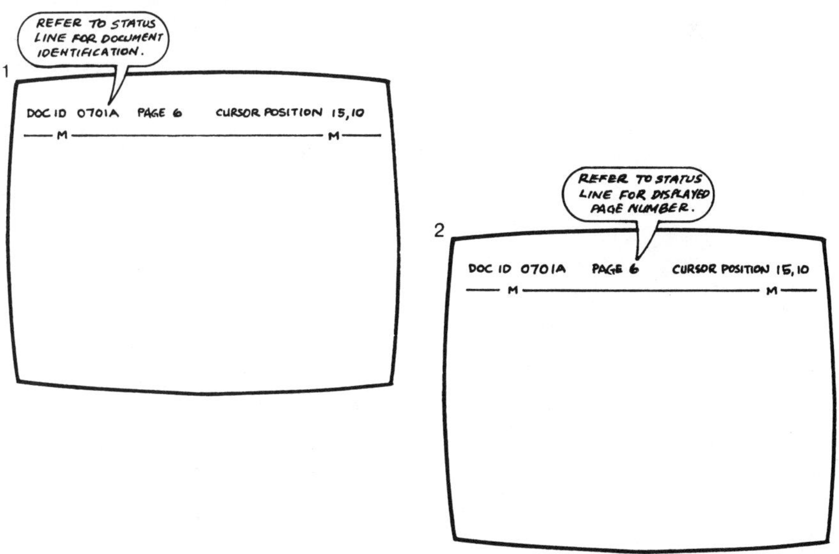

3. Determine the cursor position. Note that the cursor is on line 15, character position 10.

Module 16
FORMAT

DESCRIPTION

The format function is used to establish margins, tabs, and line spacing for a displayed document or for specified lines of text within a document. Formats are established by the system operator as documents are being created. Most systems allow multiple formats, or different margins, tab settings, and line spacing, to be contained on the same page. When establishing formats, the cursor is moved from the text area to the format line, usually located at the top or bottom of the display screen, by pressing a FORMAT key sequence.

Existing margins and tabs can be erased by moving the cursor over them and pressing the space bar or special character. New line spacing, margins, and tabs can be entered by typing the proper character at the desired position on the format line. For example, line spacing might be changed from single-space to double-space by typing a 2 over the 1 at the line-space character position. Margins can be set, say at 10 and 75, by entering a margin character, such as an *M*, and character positions 10 and 75 on the format line. Similarly, tabs can be entered by pressing the tab character, such as *T*, at the selected positions on the format line.

Once line spacing, margins, and tabs are set, an EXECUTE key sequence is pressed. This returns the cursor to the line from which it came. For example, if the cursor was on line 1 when the FORMAT key sequence was pressed, it will return to line 1. If it was on line 12, it will return to line 12.

APPLICATIONS

The format function allows the word processing system operator to set page format parameters just as on a conventional typewriter. Formats can be set for entire pages or for lines of text within a page.

TYPICAL OPERATION

In this illustration the format function will be used to set margins at character positions 20 and 65 and a tab at character position 40, with the cursor located at the beginning of line 14 of a displayed document.

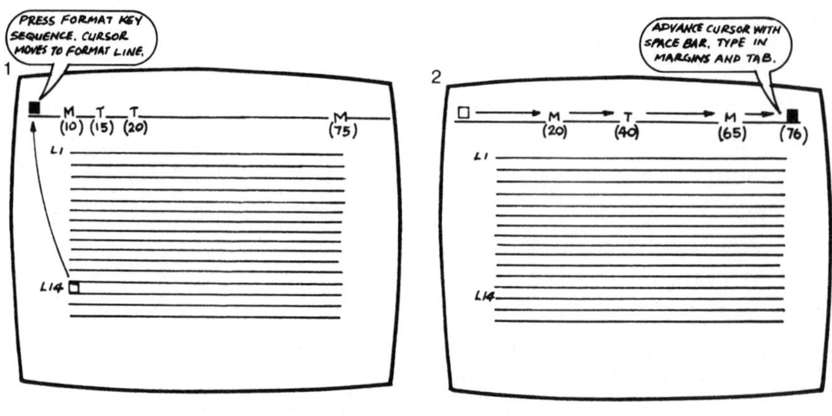

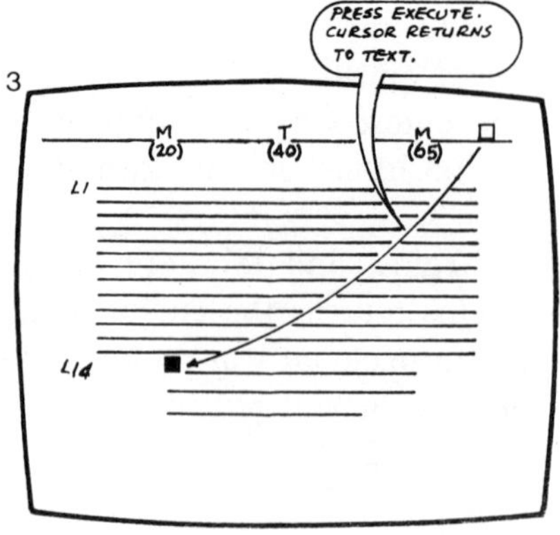

1. Move the cursor to the format line by pressing the FORMAT key sequence.

2. Using the space bar to advance the cursor, space to character position 20 and type *M*, to character position 40 and type *T*, and to character position 65 and type *M*. Note that the space bar erased the old margins and tab settings and typing *M* and *T* entered the new margins and tab.

3. Press the EXECUTE key sequence to return the cursor to the beginning of line 14.

Module 17
TAB (STANDARD)

DESCRIPTION

The standard tab function is used to set tabs on a word processing system just as on a standard typewriter. Tabs are set on the system format line as described in Module 16. Once tabs are set, the TAB key is pressed to advance the cursor to the tab character position to the right of the cursor. If no tabs are set on the format line, pressing the TAB key often advances the cursor to the right margin of the present line or left margin of the following line, depending on the word processing system being used. Other systems may display a prompt, or "error message," stating that no tabs are set.

APPLICATIONS

The tab function is used to indent the first line of new paragraphs or to indent to the first character positions in vertical columns of text. On some systems, tabs are entered to the left of the left margin to allow text entry, such as paragraph numbers, in the margin's white space.

TYPICAL OPERATION

In this illustration the tab function will be used to create a two-column table. The columns will begin at character positions 20 and 40 on line 1 of page 1 of a new document.

1. With the first page of a new document displayed, move the cursor to the format line by using the FORMAT key sequence.
2. Using the right arrow (East) key and the character T, set tabs and character positions 20 and 40 and return to line 1 by pressing the EXECUTE key sequence.
3. Using the TAB key to position the cursor to the beginning of each column, type the columns of text.

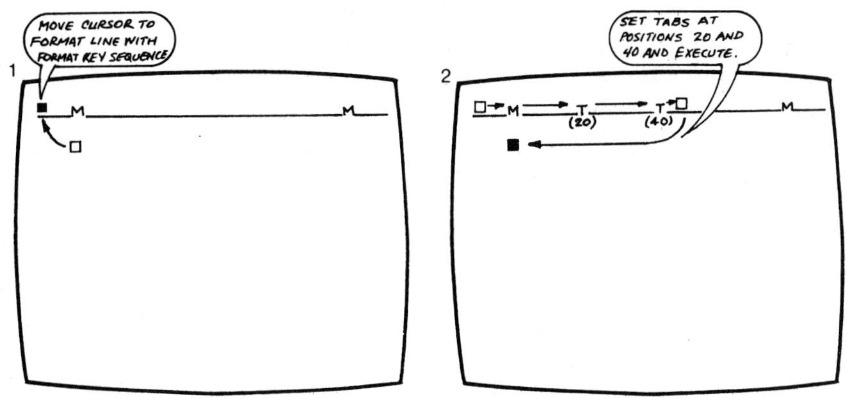

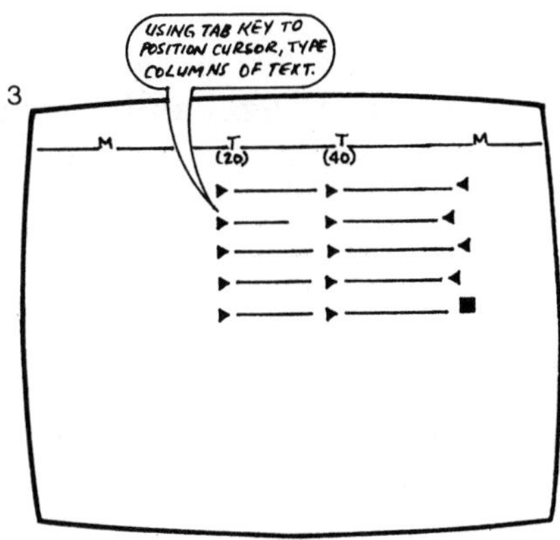

Module 18
ALIGN TAB (OR DECIMAL TAB)

DESCRIPTION

Align tabs, sometimes called "decimal" tabs, are used to type numbers containing decimals (or periods) so that regardless of the length of the number, all decimal points will be aligned in a vertical column. Some systems allow other characters to be substituted for the period character. For example, European notation uses commas instead of periods to express decimal values. Therefore it may be desirable to use a comma as the align character instead of the period.

Some systems use "combination" tabs, which can be used as either a standard or an align tab. Where used, standard or align tab selection is made by using the TAB key for standard tab selection, or a special key sequence, such as CONTROL T, for align tab selection.

When using the align tab, the text moves from right to left until the period is typed. The period aligns at the align tab position, and the following text moves from left to right until the TAB or RETURN key is pressed.

APPLICATIONS

The align tab function is normally used to align decimal points in columns of numbers containing decimal points. The function is particularly valuable where large numbers of financial documents are prepared containing dollars and cents. Another use of the align tab is to prepare text so that it adjusts "flush right." This will be described in detail in Module 21.

TYPICAL OPERATION

In this illustration the align tab function will be used in conjunction with a standard tab to create a two-column, five-line table beginning on line 1 of page 1. The standard tab column, designated by a *T*, will be entered at character position 20. The align tab, designated by an *A*, will be entered at character position 40.

1. With the first page of a new document displayed, move the cursor to the format line by using the FORMAT key sequence.

2. Set the standard tab at character position 20 and the align tab at character position 40 using the appropriate tab set key sequence (*T* and *A* in this example). Return the cursor to line 1 using the EXECUTE key sequence.

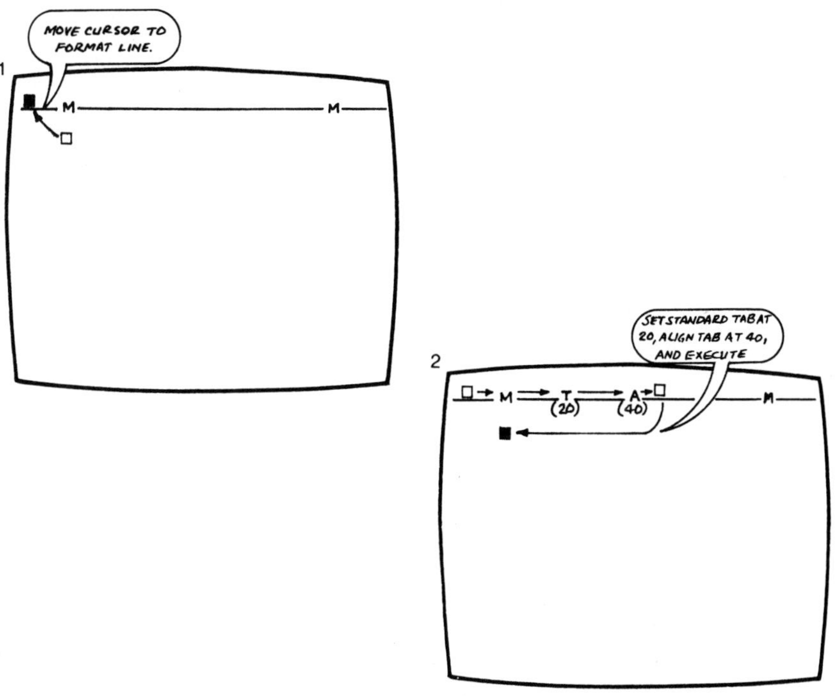

3. Using the TAB key for the first column and the ALIGN TAB key sequence for the second column, type the table entries.

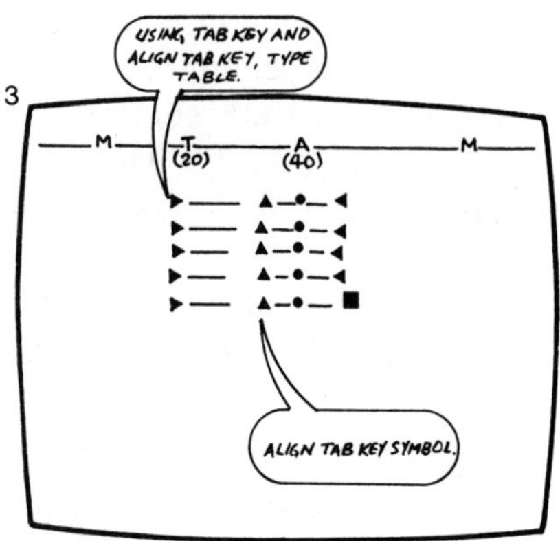

Module 19
OUTLINE TAB

DESCRIPTION

The outline tab function is used to begin a line of text at a specific character position. On some systems the outline tab is no more than a standard tab located to the left of the left margin. This allows the cursor to be advanced beyond the left margin with the TAB key sequence, and text can then be typed in the white space of the margin. Some systems use a special tab character to designate an outline tab, which may be located on either side of the left margin. On those systems that perform automatic word wrap, the RETURN key is often used to move the cursor to the outline tab position. When the outline tab is outside the left margin, the standard TAB key often advances the cursor to the left margin. In our illustration we'll use a capital *O* to designate the outline tab position on the format line.

APPLICATIONS

The outline tab function is used to type information in the margins of a document such as paragraph or procedural step numbers or letters. When the outline tab is positioned to the right of the left margin, it is often used to indent the first line of each new paragraph of text automatically. In either case, the same key sequence is used to move the cursor to the outline tab position.

TYPICAL OPERATION

In this illustration the outline tab will be used to place the numbers 1 and 2 outside the left margin in the preparation of a two-step procedure.

1. With the first page of a new document displayed, move the cursor to the format line by using the FORMAT key sequence.
2. Set an outline tab (capital *O*) at character position 5, set the left margin at character position 10 and the right margin at character position 75, and return the cursor to line 1 using the EXECUTE key sequence.
3. Press RETURN and note that the cursor moves to line 2, character position 5. Type number one period (1.), press the TAB key, type two or three lines of text for the first procedural step, and press RETURN twice to insert a blank line between steps 1 and 2.
4. Type number two period (2.), press the TAB key, and type the text of the second procedural step.

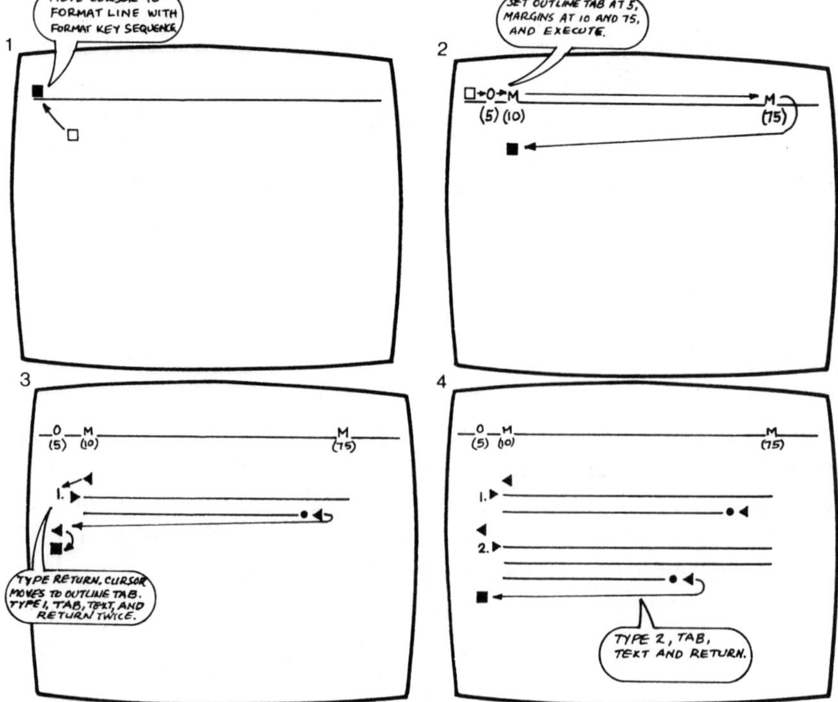

Module 20
TABULAR EDITING

DESCRIPTION

Tabular editing functions offered on many word processing systems are designed to manipulate vertical columns of text. Because most standard word processing editing features are line oriented, that is, they delete or insert horizontal lines rather than verticaal columns of text, the tabular editing features give the system operator a powerful alternative to line-at-a-time editing. The standard insert, delete, and move functions are used in conjunction with other keystrokes to achieve tabular editing. Both methods and capabilities vary widely from system to system. For example, switching columns of text may be achieved with a few simple keystrokes on one system, while another may require using the copy, move, and delete functions in combination to achieve the same results. When deleting the first column of a three-column table, some systems automatically "close up" the space vacated by the deleted column, others leave the space open (or vacant), and still others give the operator a choice of either closing up or leaving open.

Common to tabular editing is the need to identify the location of columns to be edited. The character and line positions must be defined, usually by moving the cursor to the top-left and bottom-right column coordinates, before column editing can begin.

APPLICATIONS

Tabular editing functions allow columns of text to be inserted, deleted, moved, or switched within tables, referred to as "tabular material." An example of tabular editing might be to maintain a twelve-month financial forecast table. The table, which must be updated the first of each month, contains twelve columns of numbers. Each month the left-hand column (column 1) of a twelve-column table must be deleted, columns 2 through 12 must be shifted to the left to fill the space vacated by the deleted column, and then a new column 12 must be added on the right. By using the column delete and close-up function, column 1 is defined by using the cursor and is deleted, columns 2 through 12 automatically shift left, and a new column 12 may be typed in the open space at the right.

TYPICAL OPERATION

In this illustration the first column of a three-column, five-line table will be deleted. Columns 2 and 3 will shift to the left, and a new column 3 will be typed. The columns will begin on line 1, characters 20, 40, and 60.

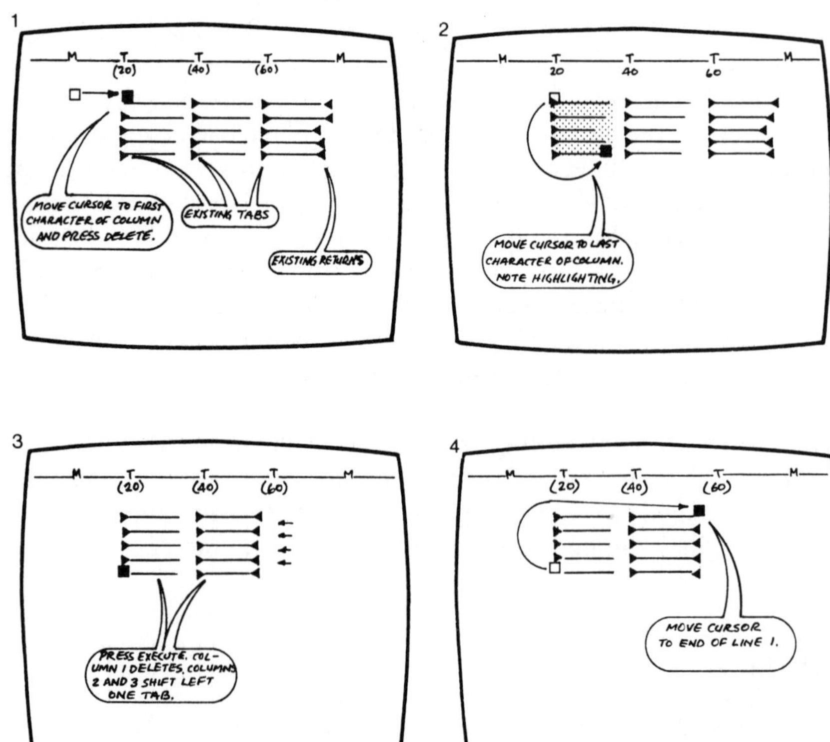

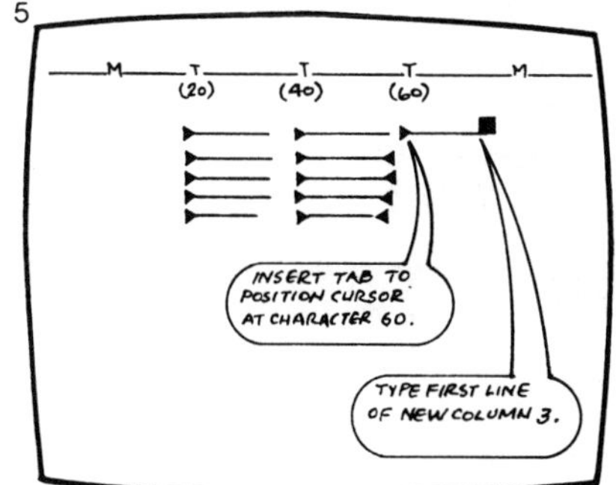

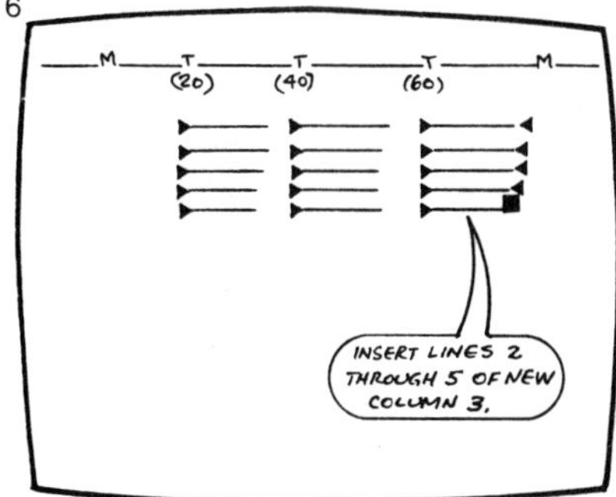

1. With the cursor on line 1, character position 1, use the right arrow (East) key to move the cursor to line 1, character 20, and press the column DELETE key sequence.

2. Using the down arrow (South) and right arrow (East) keys, move the cursor over the bottom right-hand character of column 1. Note that the text in column 1 is highlighted.

3. Verifying that the proper text is highlighted, press the EXECUTE key sequence. Note that column 1 disappears and that columns 2 and 3 shift left one tab space.

4. Using the up arrow (North) and right arrow (East) keys, move the cursor to the end of line 1 (over the RETURN symbol).

5. Using the INSERT function, press the TAB key to move the cursor to character position 60, type the first line of new column 3, and EXECUTE.

6. Repeat step 5 to insert new column 3, lines 2 through 5. Use the arrow keys for cursor positioning.

Module 21
FLUSH RIGHT (USING ALIGN TAB)

DESCRIPTION

The ALIGN TAB key sequence can be used on many word processing systems to align the right edge of a column of text so that it is smooth, or "justified," within the body of a document. This is done by pressing the ALIGN TAB key sequence, typing text without a period (which causes decimal alignment), and pressing the TAB or RETURN key. The line of text will end at the align tab position because when text is typed in conjunction with the align tab function, it moves from right to left. Each character typed is located directly in line with the align tab; previously typed characters are displaced to the left. For example, the word T H E is typed on the align tab as follows:

Type T	T
Type H	T H
Type E	T H E
	∧
	(align tab)

Note that as each character is being typed, it is automatically positioned over the align tab (∧) and the previously typed character moves to the left.

APPLICATIONS

Using the align tab without periods to prepare multiple lines of text produces a column of text with a smooth right edge and a "ragged" left edge, hence the term *flush right.*

TYPICAL OPERATION

In this illustration a five-line flush-right column will be typed using an align tab located at character position 40.

> **1.** With the first page of a new document displayed, move the cursor to the format line by using the FORMAT key sequence.
>
> **2.** Set an align tab at character position 40. Return the cursor to line 1 by using the EXECUTE key sequence.
>
> **3.** Press the ALIGN TAB key sequence, type the first line of text, and press the RETURN key. Note that the text moves to the left as it is being typed.
>
> **4.** Repeat step 3 for lines 2 through 5.

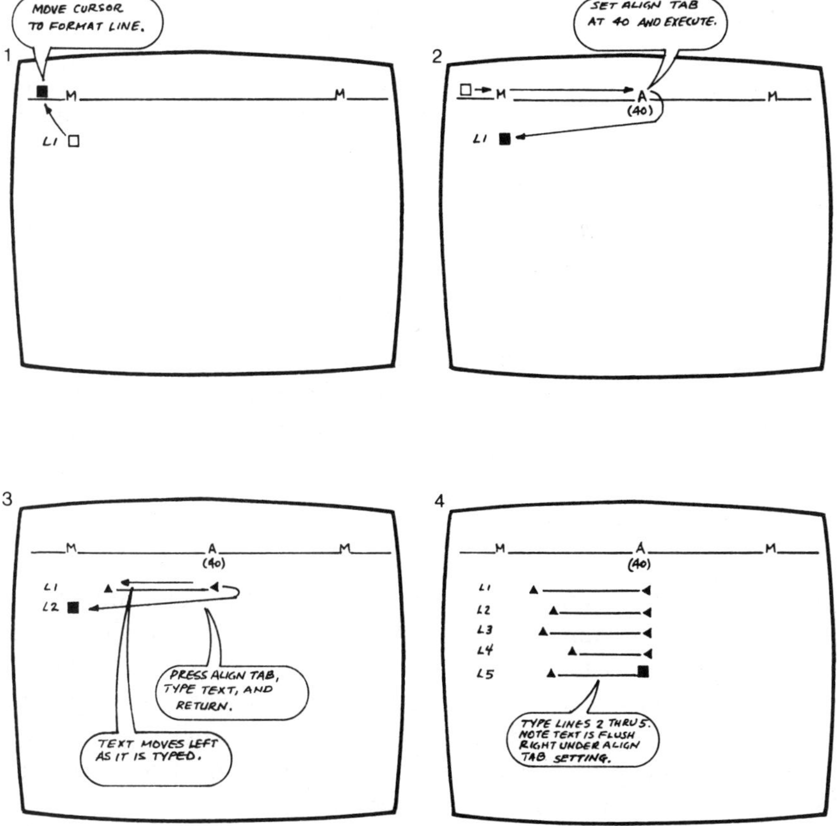

Module 22
REFORMAT

DESCRIPTION

The reformat function is used to change margins, tabs, line spacing, or the number of lines per page on an existing document. The entire document may be reformatted, or only a portion of a document may be reformatted, such as a paragraph.

Setting a new format is normally accomplished the same way as setting the original format when a document is created. The major difference is that text to be reformatted must be identified. This is normally done by pointing to the beginning and end of the text to be reformatted with the cursor and using a special REFORMAT key sequence.

The cursor must be moved to the format line in order to set the new format parameters. Once the text area is defined and the new format is established on the format line, the text can be reformatted by entering the EXECUTE key sequence.

APPLICATIONS

The reformat function can change the appearance of a document substantially. For example, a draft document may be double-spaced with wide margins to accommodate editing marks. Once editorial comments are incorporated and the document is ready to be printed in final form, the reformat function can be used to change the line spacing and margins. This is only one application of the reformat function; many more could be described.

TYPICAL OPERATION

In this illustration the reformat function will be used to change the margins of the second paragraph of a displayed page of text. The original margins will be at character positions 10 and 75. The selected paragraph's margins will be changed to character positions 20 and 65.

1. Using the down arrow (South) key, move the cursor to the first line of the second paragraph.

2. Press the REFORMAT key sequence; note that the cursor moves to the format line.

3. Set the new margins at character positions 20 and 65, and press the EXECUTE key sequence. Note that the cursor returns to the first character of the second paragraph.

4. Move the cursor to the last line of the second paragraph; note that each line of text highlights as the cursor moves down.

5. Press the EXECUTE key sequence; note that the margins of the second paragraph change to character positions 20 and 65.

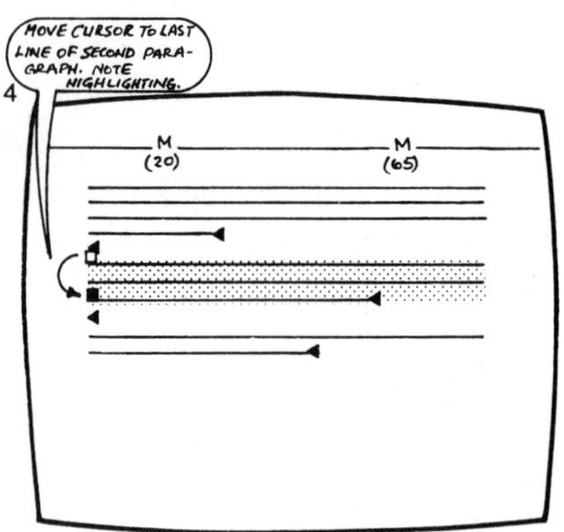

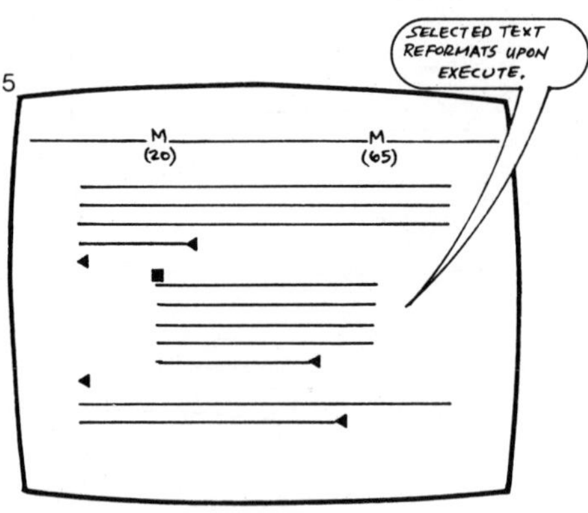

Module 23
STRIKEOVER

DESCRIPTION

The strikeover function is used to replace individual characters and spaces with other characters or spaces. When a strikeover is performed on a typewriter, the existing character is simply struck over with a new character. Both the first and second characters remain in the text. When a strikeover is performed on the display screen of a word processor, the old character is replaced by the new one. The function is performed by moving the cursor over the character or space to be struck out and typing the new one.

APPLICATIONS

The strikeover function is used to make simple corrections. It can be used to replace words as well as characters and spaces, as long as the new word is the same length as the one being struck over. When the old word is longer or shorter than the new one, the delete or insert function must be used to adjust spacing.

TYPICAL OPERATION

In this illustration the word *t e h* will be corrected to *t h e* by backspacing and typing *h e* in place of *e h*.

1. With the cursor located at the space following the *h* in *t e h*, press the BACKSPACE or left arrow (West) key twice to position the cursor over the character *e*.

2. Type the correct characters *h e.* Note that the characters *h e* replace *e h.*

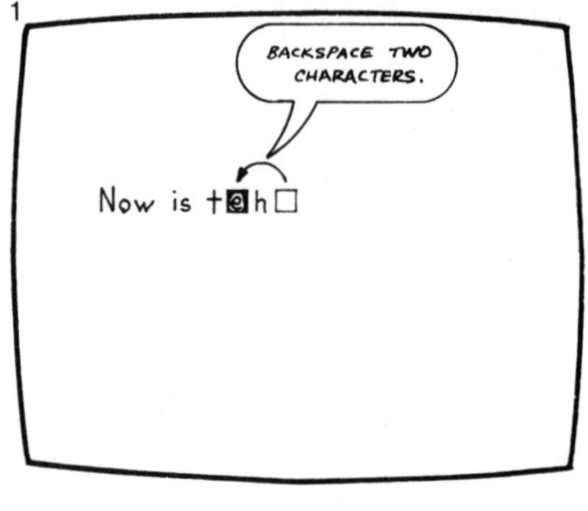

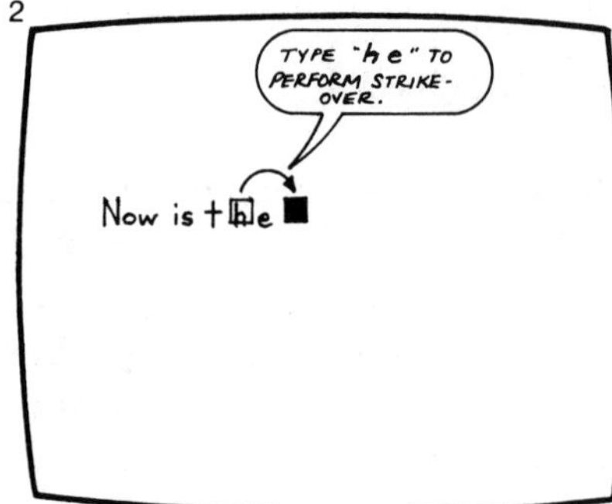

Module 24
DELETE

DESCRIPTION

The delete function is used to erase text from a displayed document or entire documents from the word processing system's storage medium. When text is deleted from a page, the following text normally "closes up," or fills the space vacated by the deleted text. Some word processing systems allow the operator to choose keeping the vacated space intact by pressing a special key sequence in combination with the DELETE key sequence. When this is done, the text that follows the deleted block remains in place. The delete function on some systems is restricted to one page at a time; others permit deletion of text on multiple pages.

To delete text within a displayed document, the cursor is used to select the beginning and end points of the text to be deleted. When the cursor is on the first character of text to be deleted, the DELETE key sequence is pressed. The cursor is then moved to the last character to be deleted. The text within the selected area highlights. The EXECUTE key sequence is pressed to complete the delete function.

APPLICATIONS

The delete function is used to erase characters, words, sentences, paragraphs, pages, or groups of pages from a displayed document. It also is used to erase entire documents from the word processing system's storage medium.

TYPICAL OPERATION

In this illustration the delete function will be used to delete the second paragraph and following blank line from a displayed document.

1. Using the down arrow (South) key, move the cursor to the first character of the second paragraph and press the DELETE key sequence.
2. Using the down arrow (South) key, move the cursor to the blank line beneath the second paragraph. Note that the identified text highlights.
3. Press the EXECUTE key sequence. Note that the selected text disappears and the following text fills in the vacated space.

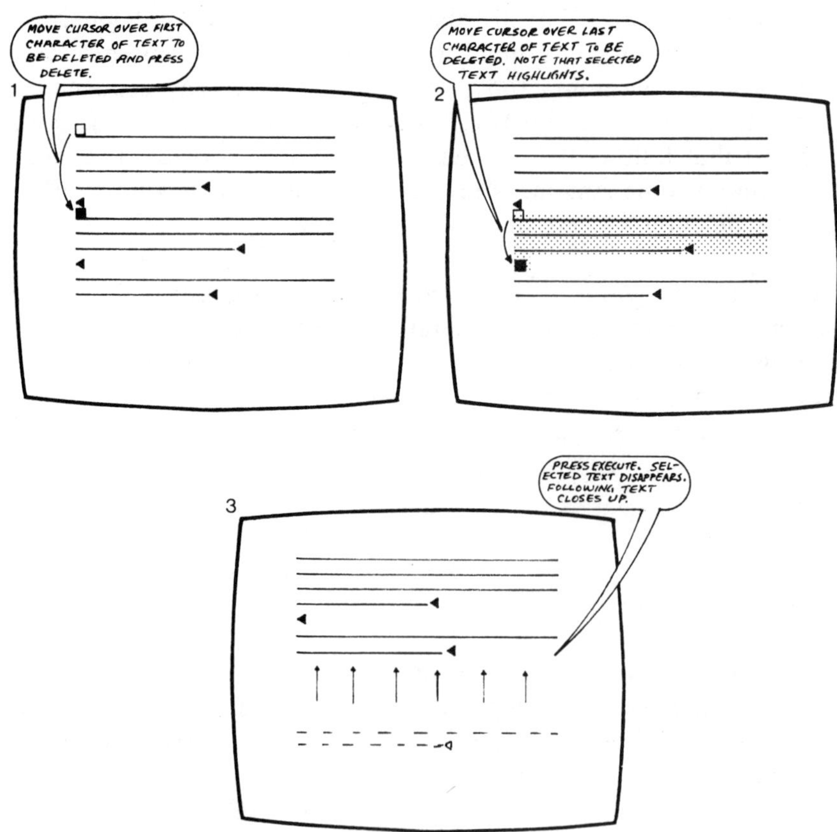

Module 25
INSERT

DESCRIPTION

The insert function is used to add new text within the existing text of a displayed document. The insert function relocates the following text to the right and down as the new text is being typed. When a new page is inserted, the following page numbers are normally incremented to the next higher number automatically. For example, if a new page is inserted between pages 1 and 2 of a document, the new page becomes 2 and the following page, formerly page 2, becomes 3.

Some systems insert pages by giving them the prior page number with an extension number. Using the example above, the inserted page might be numbered 1.1. The sequence, then, would be pages 1, 1.1, and 2.

The insert function is accomplished by positioning the cursor to the location where inserted text is to begin, pressing the INSERT key sequence. This moves the following text to the right and down to make room for the text to be inserted. Next, the new text is typed; the following text will continue to move out of the way. Once all the inserted text has been typed, the EXECUTE key sequence is pressed and the following text closes up to the cursor position.

APPLICATIONS

The insert function is used to insert characters, words, sentences, paragraphs, and pages within a displayed document.

TYPICAL OPERATION

In this illustration the insert function will be used to insert a new sentence between the first and the second sentence of a displayed document.

1. Using the right arrow (East) key, move the cursor over the first character of the second sentence.

2. Press the INSERT key sequence and note that the following text moves to the right and down, leaving space to insert new text.

3. Type the new sentence including the period and following space. Note that text highlights as it is being inserted.

4. Press the EXECUTE key sequence. Note that the following text closes up.

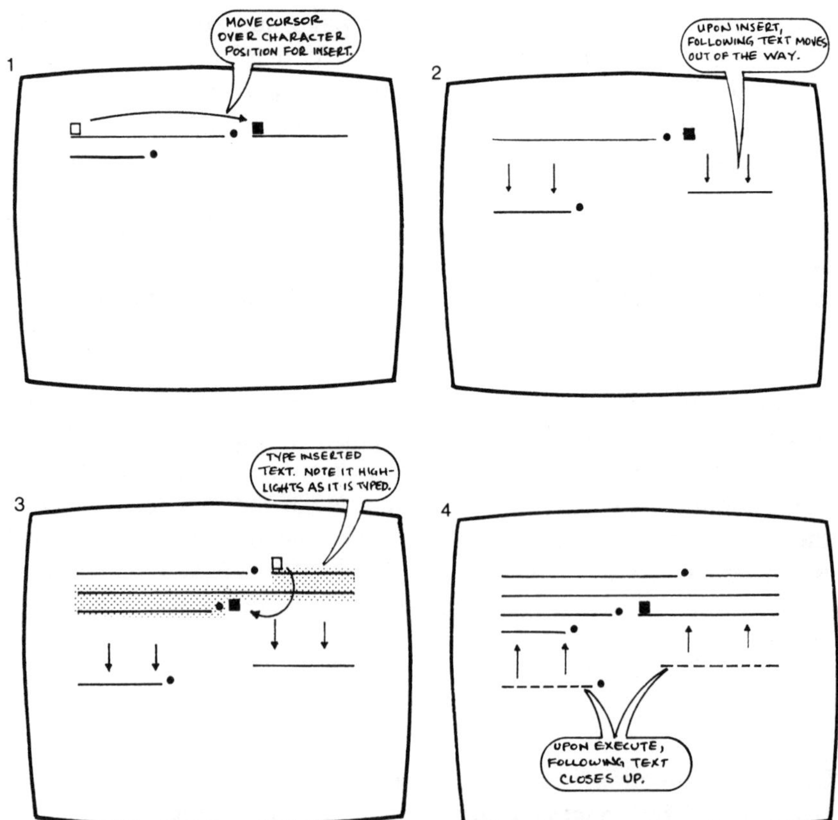

Module 26
MOVE

DESCRIPTION

The move function is used to move text from one location to another. This function, sometimes called "block move," can move text in several ways. This includes moving text from one location to another on the same page, to a different page, or to a different document.

The move function causes the selected text to be taken from its original location. When gone, the text following the original location "closes up" the space vacated by the moved text. Using the cursor, the operator selects the point in the displayed document where the moved text is to reappear. Upon execution, the moved text reappears. When it reappears, it displaces the following text to the right and down.

APPLICATIONS

The move function is used to relocate characters, words, sentences, paragraphs, pages, groups of pages, and even entire documents from one location to another. The alternative to move would be to delete text from one location of a document and reenter it in another.

TYPICAL OPERATION

In this illustration the second paragraph and the following blank line will be moved above the first paragraph.

1. Using the down arrow (South) key, position the cursor over the first character of the text to be moved and press the MOVE key sequence.

2. Using the down arrow (South) key, position the cursor over the last character to be moved, in this case the blank line following the second paragraph. Note that the selected text highlights.

3. Press the EXECUTE key sequence. Note that the selected text disappears (stored in the system's memory), and the following text fills in the vacated space.

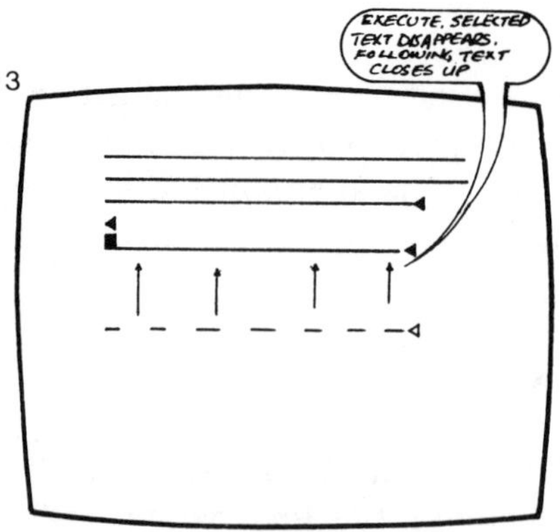

4. Using the up arrow (North) key, place the cursor over the character position where the selected text is to be recalled.
5. Press the EXECUTE key sequence; selected text reappears. Displaced text readjusts automatically.

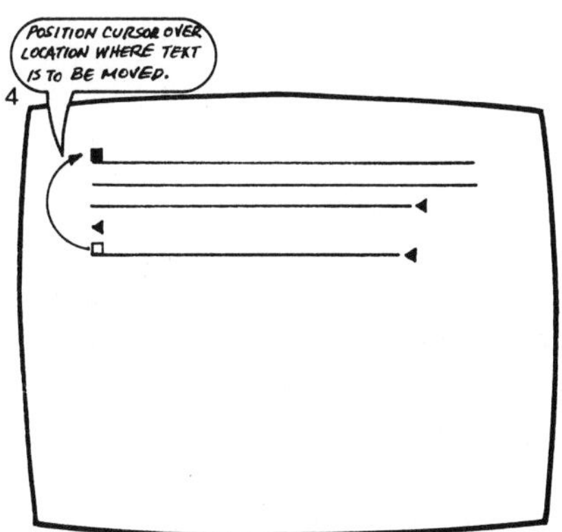

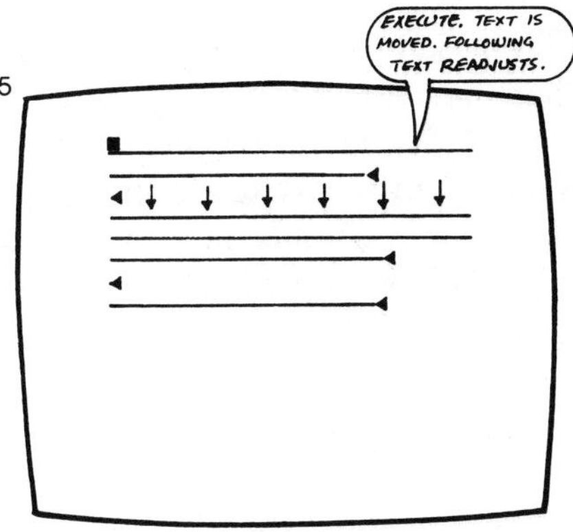

Module 27
COPY (OR DUPLICATE)

DESCRIPTION

The copy function is used to duplicate existing text in other locations. This function can duplicate selected passages of text at other locations on the same page of a displayed document, on other pages of a displayed document, or in other documents.

The copy function is accomplished by placing the cursor over the first character of the selected text to be duplicated and pressing the COPY key sequence. The cursor is then moved over the last character of text to be duplicated. The selected text highlights. When the EXECUTE key sequence is pressed, a copy of the selected text is stored in the system's memory. The original text is not affected. Next, the cursor is moved to the character position at which the text is to be copied. Upon the EXECUTE key sequence, the text appears, displacing the following text to the right and down.

APPLICATIONS

The copy function is used to reproduce existing characters, words, sentences, paragraphs, pages, or entire documents. The alternative to copy would be to retype entire passages of text by using the insert function. Of course, where passages are short, rekeyboarding may be easier.

TYPICAL OPERATION

In this illustration the copy function will be used to duplicate the first three lines of text on page 1 of a displayed document to the top of page 2 of the same document.

1. With the cursor positioned at the first character of the first line of page 1, press the COPY key sequence.

2. Using the down arrow (South) and right arrow (East) keys, move the cursor over the last character of the third line. Note that the selected text highlights.

3. Press the EXECUTE key sequence and note that the highlight disappears. (The selected text stays in place.)

4. Using the GO TO PAGE 2 key sequence, display page 2 and press the EXECUTE key sequence. Note that the selected text is copied to the first three lines of page 2.

Module 28
CENTER

DESCRIPTION

The center function is used to center a horizontal line of text between the left and right margins of a document. Some systems allow centering over a selected character location on a horizontal line. The centering function is activated in different ways on different systems. On some, the CENTER key sequence is entered prior to text entry. Others require text entry first and then CENTER key sequence entry. In either case, the cursor must be positioned on the line being centered. When centering over a selected point, the cursor must be located on the character position, the CENTER key sequence entered, and the text typed. The text will "spread" a character at a time to either side of the cursor position so that it centers over the selected point.

APPLICATIONS

The centering function is used to horizontally center such things as illustration and table titles and chapter headings either above or below the corresponding text. On those systems that allow text to be centered over a selected character position, headings can be made to center over vertical columns of text, as in tables.

TYPICAL OPERATION

In this illustration the center function will be used to center a title on the first line of the displayed document.

1. With the cursor at the left margin of line 1, page 1, press the CENTER key sequence. Note that the cursor moves to the center of the blank line.

2. Type the title. Note that it spreads to either side of the original cursor position.

3. Upon entering the last character of the title, press RETURN; the cursor moves to the left margin of the next line.

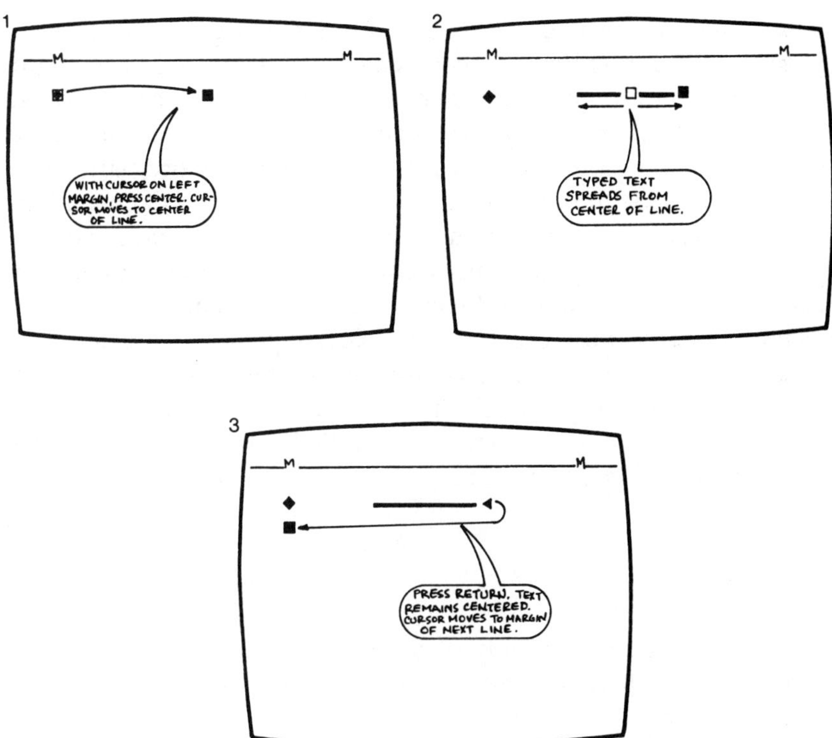

Module 29
INDENT

DESCRIPTION

The indent function is used to move the left margin of a block of text, such as a paragraph, to a character position located to the right of the outside left margin. When only one line of text is to be indented, such as indenting five spaces at the beginning of a new paragraph, a standard tab can be used. Where an entire paragraph is to be indented, the indent function is used. Most systems allow multiple levels of indentation. These commonly have special INDENT keys or key sequences and use tab locations as indent locations. Using the indent function is very similar to using the standard tab function. The INDENT key sequence is pressed and text is typed except that instead of having the following lines of text begin at the original left margin, they return to the indent position until the indent function is canceled. Many systems cancel the indent function by pressing the RETURN key.

APPLICATIONS

The indent function is typically used for outline levels and paragraph subordination, where indentation is used to indicate subordinate paragraph levels.

TYPICAL OPERATION

In this illustration the indent function will be used to prepare three two-line paragraphs. The first paragraph will begin at the left margin, the second at character position 5, and the third at character position 10. The indent function will use standard tab positions.

1. With the first page of a new document displayed, move the cursor to the format line by using the FORMAT key sequence.
2. Set a tab at character positions 5 and 10, and return the cursor to line 1 using the EXECUTE key sequence.
3. Type the first two lines of text, ending the second line with a RETURN. Note that the cursor returns to the left margin of line 3.

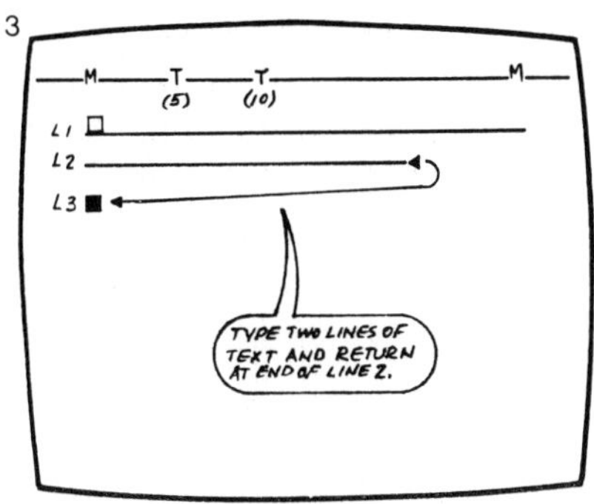

4. Beginning on line 3, press the INDENT key sequence once to advance the cursor to character position 5 and type two lines of text ending the second line (line 4) with a RETURN. Note that the cursor returns to the left margin of line 5.

5. Beginning on line 5, press the INDENT key sequence twice to advance the cursor to character position 10, and type two lines of text ending the second line (line 6) with a RETURN. Note that the cursor returns to the left margin of line 7.

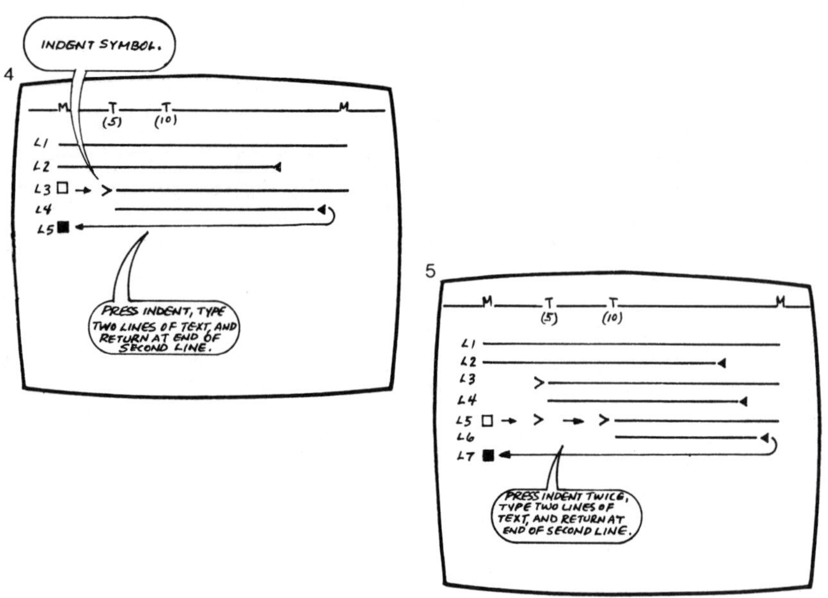

Module 30

SCROLLING (HORIZONTAL AND VERTICAL)

DESCRIPTION

Scrolling allows the operator to "roll" text up and down or from side to side on the display screen by using the cursor control keys. When the document is wider or longer than the display screen, it must be scrolled from side to side to see an entire line of text or from top to bottom to see an entire page.

Some systems scroll smoothly, a character or line at a time. Others scroll in increments of text, such as eight horizontal characters at a time or a "screenload" of twenty-two lines at a time when moving text vertically.

The horizontal scrolling function is used to prepare documents that are wider than the screen image area. For example, if a screen displays only 80 characters at a time, scrolling allows the text to move from right to left enabling the operator to continue typing in excess of the 80-character screen limitation. There are systems that scroll horizontally up to 250 characters. These systems can be used with extra-wide printers to prepare 15- to 20-inch-wide tables or charts.

The vertical scrolling function is used to move text up and down on the screen for continuous viewing. Many partial-page display screens show less than twenty-five lines of text at a time. To see the entire page, the operator must move the cursor up or down by using the up arrow (North) or down arrow (South) key sequence.

APPLICATION

The scrolling function allows an operator to view blocks of text that are larger than the display screen image area in a continuous fashion. This is similar to viewing passing information through a window.

TYPICAL OPERATION

In this illustration a line of text will be typed from the left margin to character position 96.

> **1.** With the margins set at 10 and 107 and the cursor located at the left margin, type the above sentence of text on one line. (It contains 96 characters including the period.)
>
> **2.** Note that the text moves from right to left when the words "to character position 96." are typed. This is horizontal scrolling.

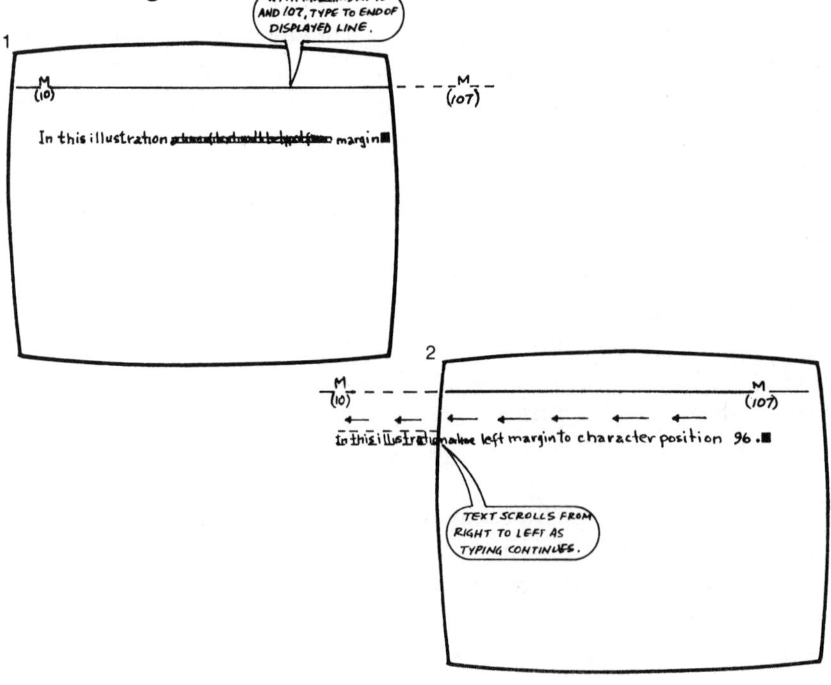

Module 31

GO TO PAGE, GET

DESCRIPTION

The go to page, or get, function is used to instruct the word processing system to move the cursor to a location on the displayed page or to display a page within a document. Some systems use different names for this function, but fundamentally they are all used to move from point to point or page to page within a document.

The go to page, or get, function normally uses a prescribed key sequence. When moving from page to page, for example, the key sequence may simply be pressing a code key labeled "GO TO PAGE," the page number, and the EXECUTE key sequence. When moving to the bottom of a displayed page, the key sequence may be pressing the GO TO PAGE key and the down arrow (South) key.

If the system uses mnemonics, that is, combinations of keys rather than labeled code keys, the key sequence may be "CONTROL G," the page number, and the EXECUTE key sequence. The CONTROL G sequence is essentially telling the system to "GET PAGE." Some systems use a "HOME" key which moves the cursor to the left margin of the first line on the displayed page. Others allow an arrow key to be used in conjunction with the home key to move the cursor to the bottom, right, or left.

APPLICATIONS

The go to page, or get, function is used to display another page within the document being edited or to move the cursor to the top, bottom, right margin, or left margin of a displayed page. Some systems allow the cursor to be moved to a specific line by using the line number in conjunction with the GO TO PAGE key sequence. The function speeds up access by eliminating the need to move the cursor a line at a time or working through a document a page at a time to go from page 1 to page 20. In this respect, the go to page function is a time saver.

TYPICAL OPERATION

In this illustration page 1 of a document will be displayed. We'll move to page 3 of the document and then to the bottom of the page.

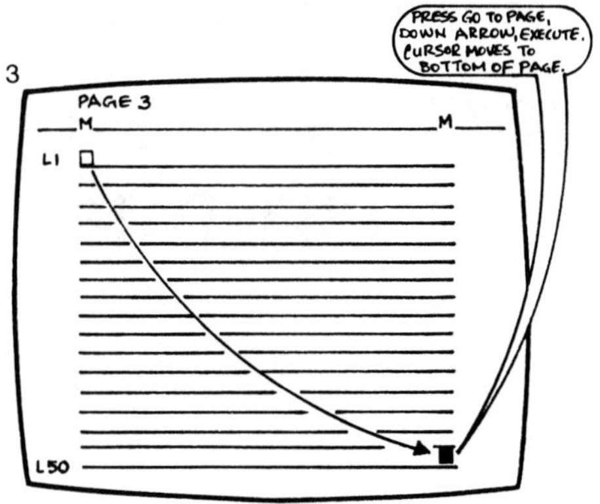

1. With page 1 displayed, press the GO TO PAGE key sequence, 3, and the EXECUTE key sequence.

2. Note that page 3 is displayed. (In the illustration, page 3 has fifty lines.)

3. Press the GO TO PAGE key sequence, the down arrow (South) key, and the EXECUTE key sequence. Note that the cursor is on the last character of page 3. (In the illustration, page 3 has fifty lines.)

Module 32

NOTE (OR RETURN TO A SPECIFIED POSITION)

DESCRIPTION

The note, or return to a specified position, function is used to return to a specific point within a document by pressing a short key sequence, which establishes a reference point to which the cursor will automatically return upon operator command.

The note function allows an operator to mark a specific point within a document and then view other portions of the document on the same or different pages. When the operator wishes to return to the mark, he or she simply presses the GO TO PAGE and NOTE key sequence, which places the cursor on the mark.

Not all word processing systems are equipped with this function, and returning to a specific position on a page requires remembering the page and cursor position. To return to the exact position on these systems, the GO TO PAGE key sequence and cursor control keys must be used.

APPLICATIONS

The note function is primarily a timesaver. It allows an operator to return to the specified point rapidly, without having to search it out by first finding the page and then the location within the page.

TYPICAL OPERATION

In this illustration a mark will be established on page 3, line 5, character 10. The operator will look at text at the bottom of page 2 and will then return to the mark using the NOTE key sequence.

> **1.** With the cursor on page 3, line 5, character 10, press the NOTE key sequence to establish a mark. On some systems, note that a special symbol is inserted at the mark.
>
> **2.** Press the GO TO PAGE, 2, and down arrow (South) key sequence in order to view the text at the bottom of page 2.
>
> **3.** Return to the mark established in step 1 by pressing the GO TO PAGE and NOTE key sequences. Cursor automatically returns to page 3, line 5, character 10.

Module 33
SEARCH (OR FIND)

DESCRIPTION

The search function is used to find a specific character string (unique character sequence) within the text. Depending on the word processing system, the search feature may be restricted to a page at a time, or it may search an entire document for the character string. When the system locates the first occurrence of a specified character string, the system may either move the cursor to it or highlight the string, making it easy to view on the displayed page. When searching for a character string on some systems, the operator may be able to select the size of the search area. For example, the search may be from the cursor location to the bottom of the page, from the cursor location to the end of the document, or from the beginning of page 1 to the end of the last page of the document.

Some systems use a specified key sequence and prompts in conjunction with the search function. Others use menus in which the operator may specify the character string, the size of the search area, and whether or not to stop at each occurrence or simply search and count every occurrence within the document. When an entire document is searched for a character string, it is commonly called "global search."

APPLICATIONS

The search function can be used for many purposes. Anytime an operator or an author wants to check a certain word, name, or number, the search function can quickly find it.

TYPICAL OPERATION

In this illustration the search function will be used to locate the first occurrence of the character string ACME on a displayed page.

1. With the cursor located over the first character of page 1 of the displayed document, press the SEARCH key sequence and note the prompt "Search for What?"

2. Type A C M E and note that the cursor moves to *A* and then *AC* and finally the entire character string *ACME* as it is being typed.

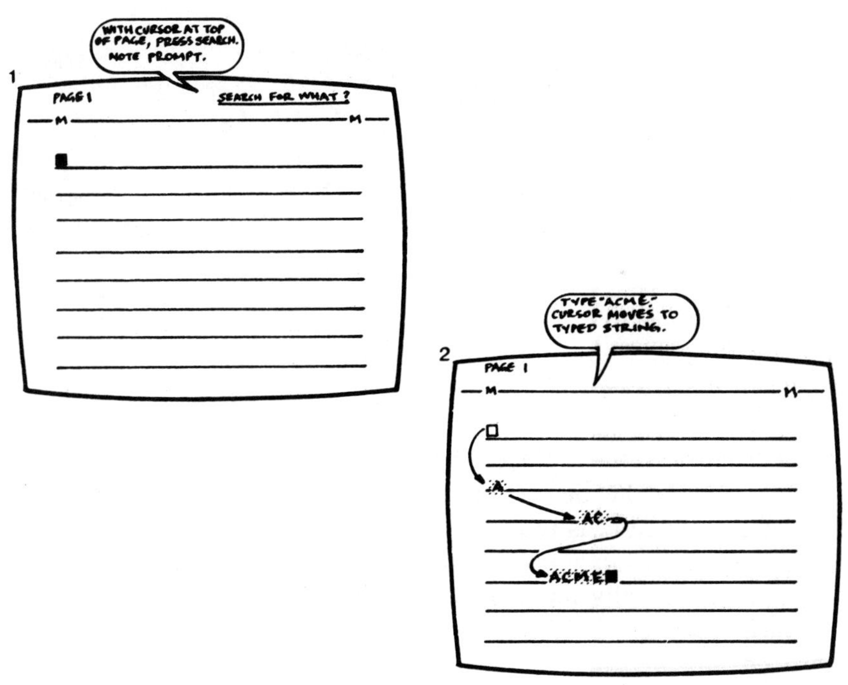

Module 34
REPLACE

DESCRIPTION

The replace function is used to replace a specified character string with another. The replace function uses either screen prompts or menus. When using a screen prompt system, the cursor is normally placed over the first character of the character string to be replaced and a REPLACE key sequence is entered. Next, the cursor is advanced to the last character of the selected string and the EXECUTE key sequence is pressed. The selected character string disappears and a new character string is typed. Finally, the EXECUTE key sequence is entered to complete the replace function.

Menus combine the replace function with the search function, performing search and replace in combination. This is described in the next module.

An alternative to the replace function would be to simply strike over the text or use the delete and insert functions. The advantage to the replace function is that it takes fewer keystrokes than using the delete and insert functions in combination. In addition, the following text is automatically adjusted as in insert or delete when the new character string is longer or shorter than the string being replaced.

APPLICATIONS

The replace function is used to replace words, names, or numbers with other words, names, or numbers. For example, the replace function can be used to change names, addresses, and dates on a standard letter or contract document to make it reusable.

TYPICAL OPERATION

In this illustration the replace function will be used to replace the misspelled word *TEH* with *THE.*

1. Using the arrow keys, move the cursor over the first character (*T*) of the string *T E H* to be replaced.

2. Press the REPLACE key sequence, and note the prompt "REPLACE WHAT?"

3. Using the right arrow (East) key, advance the cursor to the last character *(H)* of the string *T E H* to be replaced and press the EXECUTE key sequence. Note the prompt "REPLACE WITH WHAT?"

4. Type *T H E* and press the EXECUTE key sequence. Note that the new string *T H E* has replaced *T E H.*

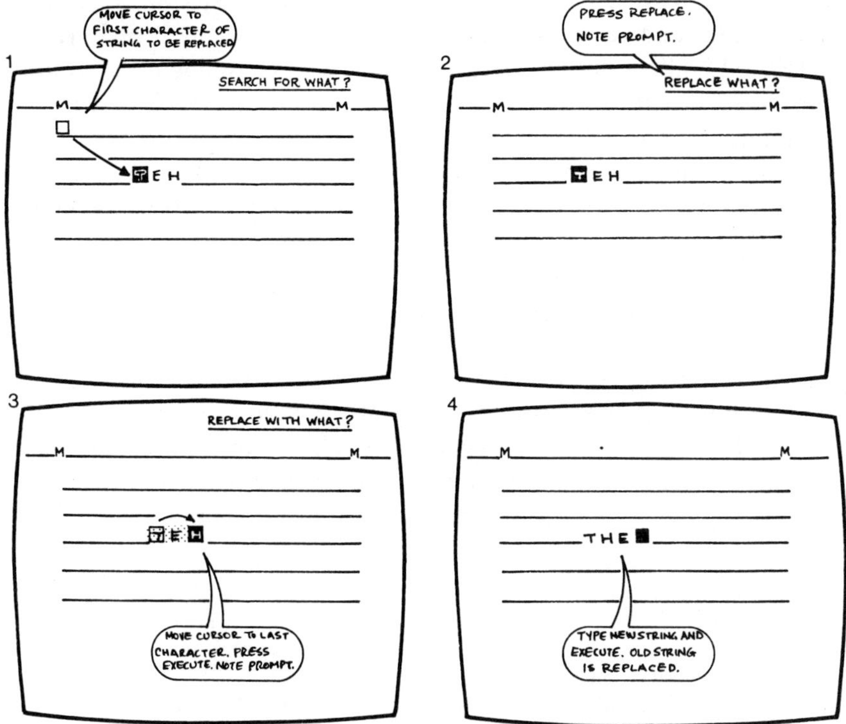

Module 35
SEARCH AND REPLACE

DESCRIPTION

The search and replace function works like the search function. It is used to search for a specified character string and replace it with another. Depending on the word processing system, the search and replace feature may be restricted to all occurrences of the specified character string on a single page, or it may search and replace every occurrence in an entire document, called "global search and replace." When the first occurrence of a specified character string is located, the system may either move the cursor to it or highlight the string and give the operator the option of replacing it, finding the next occurrence, or canceling the search and replace function to return to normal editing. Just as in the search function, some systems allow the operator to select the size of the replace area. For example, character string replacement may be from the cursor location to the bottom of the page, from the cursor location to the end of the document, or from the beginning of page 1 to the end of the last page of the document.

Some systems use a specified key sequence and prompts in conjunction with the search and replace function. Others use menus in which the operator may specify the character string, the size of the search area, and whether or not to stop at each occurrence or simply replace every occurrence within the document.

APPLICATIONS

The search and replace function is commonly used to locate and replace words, names, or numbers with other words, names, or numbers. For example, the replace function can be used to change names, addresses, and dates on a standard letter or contract document to make it reusable.

TYPICAL OPERATION

In this illustration the search and replace function will be used to search for the name *SMITH* and replace it with *JONES* on a displayed page of a document.

> **1.** With the cursor located over the first character of page 1, press the SEARCH key sequence and note the prompt "SEARCH FOR WHAT?"
>
> **2.** Type *S M I T H* and note that the cursor moves to the first occurrence. Press the REPLACE key sequence and note the prompt "REPLACE IT WITH?"

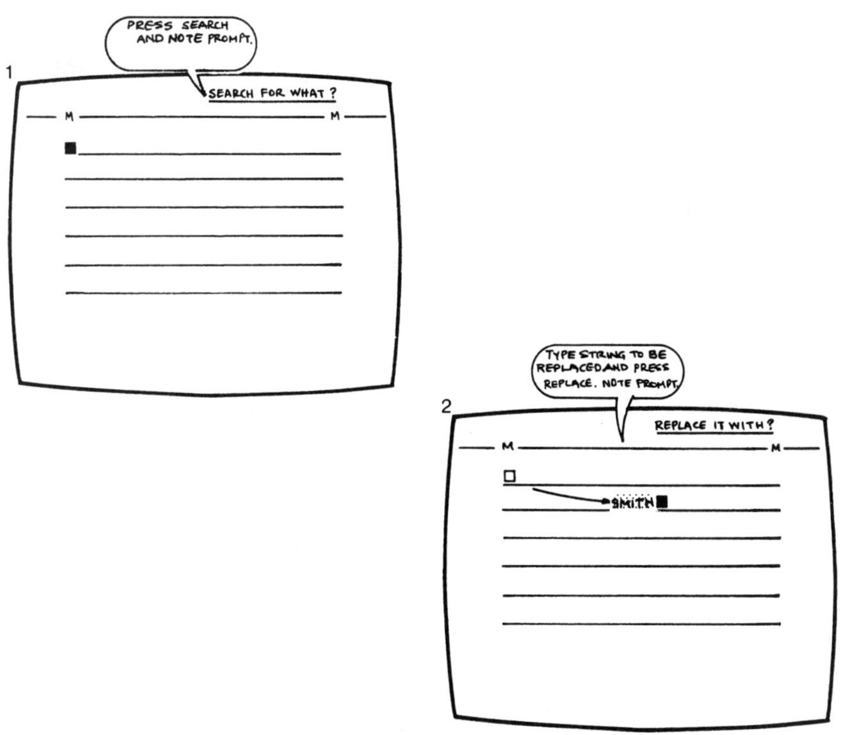

3. Type *J O N E S* and note that it appears in the screen prompt area. Press the global SEARCH and REPLACE and EXECUTE key sequences; note that all occurrences of *S M I T H* are replaced with *J O N E S*.

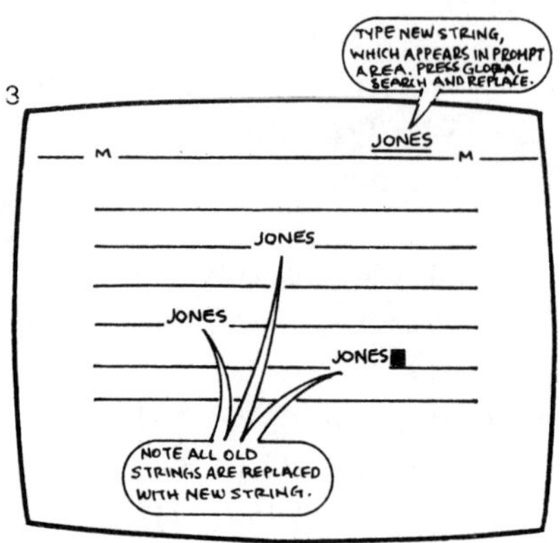

Module 36
SORT

DESCRIPTION

The sort function is used to arrange lists of words, numbers, or combinations of words and numbers (called "alphanumeric" character strings) in either ascending (low to high) or descending (high to low) order. This function operates on characters typed on a tab or multiple tab locations. When only one column of characters may be sorted at a time by a word processing system, the function is referred to as a "single-variable" sort. When two or more columns can be sorted simultaneously, it is called a "multiple-variable" sort. Although the sort function keys on a specified column, the entire line of text moves with the sorted column.

The single-variable (or column) sort is achieved by moving the cursor to the upper-left-hand character of the column to be sorted and entering the SORT key sequence. On systems allowing ascending or descending and multiple-variable sorting, the option is given to the operator either through a menu or through system prompts. Once the operator responds with the proper key sequences, the involved lines of text are rearranged, adjusting the selected columns in either ascending or descending order.

Multiple-variable sorts have primary and secondary sort columns. The primary sort column arranges each line in alphanumeric order. Secondary columns are arranged in alphanumeric order within the confines of the primary column. For example, the following two columns show primary and secondary sorting; column 1 is the primary sort column, and column 2 is the secondary sort column.

	Column 1	Column 2
Line 1	Apple	223
Line 2	Apple	224
Line 3	Grape	115
Line 4	Grape	116
Line 5	Pear	009

Note that the entries in column 1 ascend in alphabetical order, while the entries in column 2 ascend in numerical order within the boundaries of column 1.

APPLICATIONS

The sort function can be used to alphabetize names, employee numbers, zip codes, ages, salaries, and any other information arranged in columns. Sorting personnel files by name or service date is a typical application. Another valuable application is using the sort function to arrange indexes in alphabetical order. The list of names on a distribution list are often arranged by using the sort function. All of these are common uses and save many hours of valuable time.

TYPICAL OPERATION

In this illustration the sort function will be used to arrange a five-line column of names in alphabetical order. The sort will begin on line 2 of the displayed page.

1. Using the down arrow (South) and right arrow (East) keys, move the cursor to the first character of the first column.

2. Press the SORT key sequence, and note that the prompt "ASCENDING Y/N?" is displayed. (Y/N means yes or no.)

3. Type *Y* for yes to specify ascending. Note the prompt "SECONDARY SORT Y/N?"

4. Type *N* for no to specify no secondary sort column, press the EXECUTE key sequence, and note that the document is rearranged so that column 1 is in alphabetical order.

1

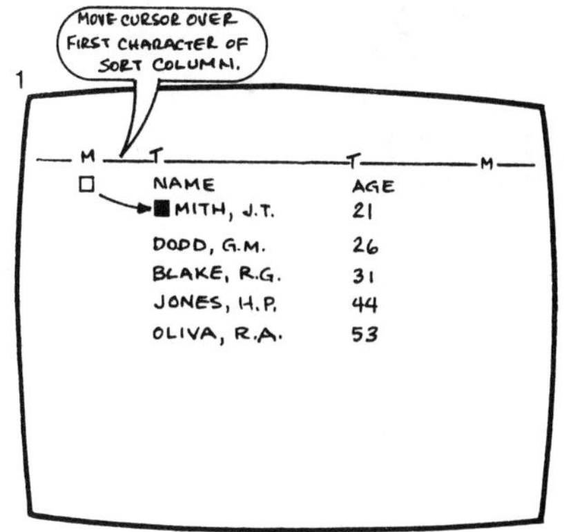
MOVE CURSOR OVER FIRST CHARACTER OF SORT COLUMN.
M T T M
NAME AGE
SMITH, J.T. 21
DODD, G.M. 26
BLAKE, R.G. 31
JONES, H.P. 44
OLIVA, R.A. 53

2

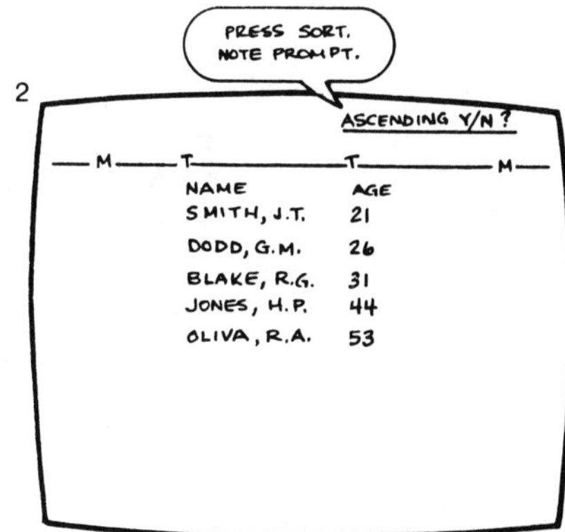
PRESS SORT. NOTE PROMPT.
ASCENDING Y/N ?
M T T M
NAME AGE
SMITH, J.T. 21
DODD, G.M. 26
BLAKE, R.G. 31
JONES, H.P. 44
OLIVA, R.A. 53

3

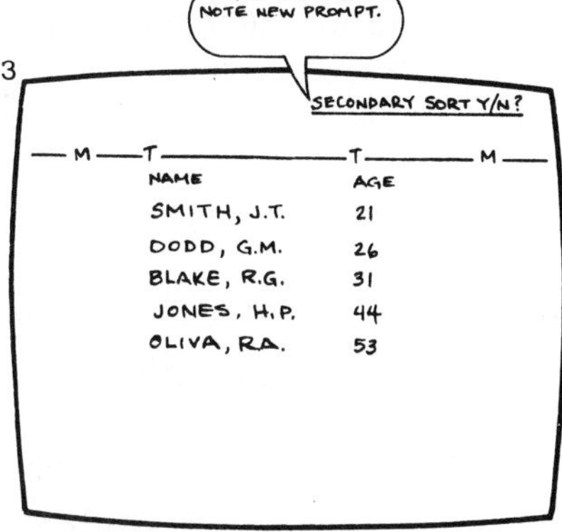
TYPE Y FOR YES. NOTE NEW PROMPT.
SECONDARY SORT Y/N ?
M T T M
NAME AGE
SMITH, J.T. 21
DODD, G.M. 26
BLAKE, R.G. 31
JONES, H.P. 44
OLIVA, R.A. 53

4

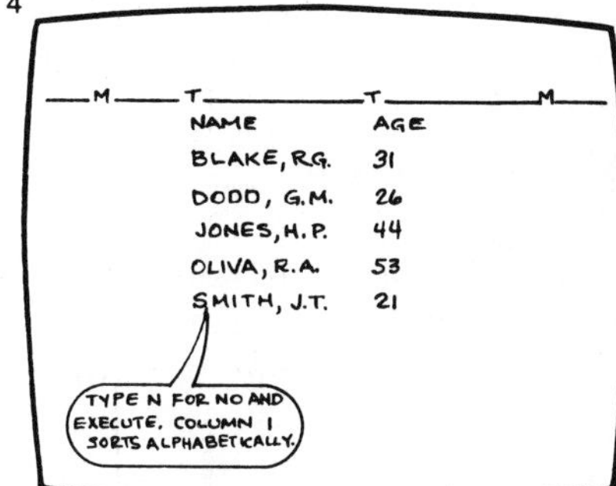
M T T M
NAME AGE
BLAKE, R.G. 31
DODD, G.M. 26
JONES, H.P. 44
OLIVA, R.A. 53
SMITH, J.T. 21
TYPE N FOR NO AND EXECUTE. COLUMN 1 SORTS ALPHABETICALLY.

Module 37
REPAGINATE

DESCRIPTION

The repaginate function is used to change the number of lines per page within a document automatically. The repaginate function is performed by initiating the repaginate function through a REPAGINATE key sequence, and responding to either repaginate menus or prompts.

APPLICATIONS

The repaginate function can be used to compensate for changes in margins or line spacing as a result of reformatting a document. Reformats will normally change page lengths. Wider margins reduce the number of lines per page; narrower margins add lines to a page.

The repaginate function can also be used to adjust newly created document pages to uniform lengths. For example, if a six-page document is created using twenty-five lines per page, it may be repaginated to fifty lines per page. The six twenty-five-line pages would reduce to three fifty-line pages.

TYPICAL OPERATION

In this illustration the repaginate function will be used to change four forty-line pages to three fifty-five-line pages.

1. With the first page of the document displayed, press the REPAGINATE key sequence. Note that a repaginate menu appears.
2. Respond to menu specifying fifty-five lines per page by typing 55 on the proper menu line.
3. Press the EXECUTE key sequence. After repagination, check to see that pages are adjusted to fifty-five lines.

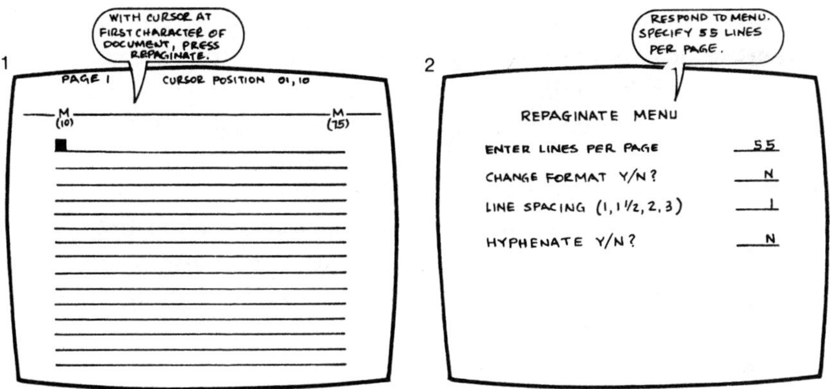

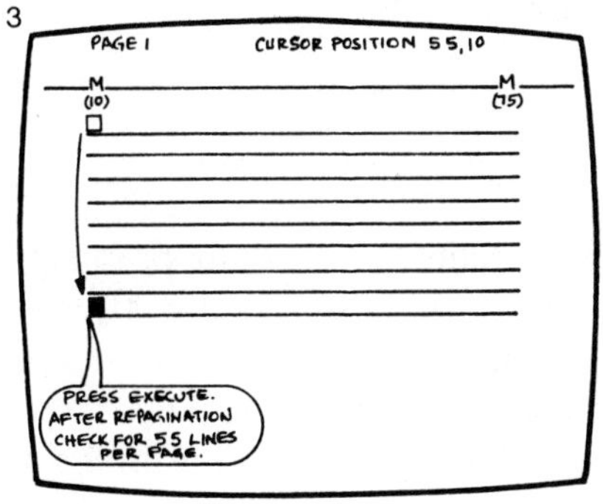

Module 38
BLOCK PROTECT

DESCRIPTION

The block protect function, sometimes called "page protect," prevents reformatting of a specified text area. Even though an entire document may be reformatted with new margins, tabs, and line spacing, the protected block of text remains unchanged.

The beginning and end points of the block of text to be protected are identified with the cursor in conjunction with the entry of a special BLOCK PROTECT key sequence. On most systems, the block protect function may be reversed by simply entering the same key sequence initially used to protect it.

The alternative to block protect would be to reformat a document selectively. All text preceding the block would first be reformatted, and then the text following the text would be reformatted, leaving the block unchanged.

APPLICATIONS

The block protect function is used to preserve special text areas, such as tables and charts, from being affected by the reformat function. If a document is reformatted and complex tables are unprotected, they may be "scrambled" by the reformat. As a result, the operator may find it very time consuming when attempting to recreate the complex tables in their original form.

TYPICAL OPERATION

In this illustration the block protect function will be used to preserve a table located in the middle of a displayed page.

1. Using the down arrow (South) key, move the cursor to the first line of the table to be protected.
2. Enter the BLOCK PROTECT key sequence, and move the cursor to the last line of the table to be protected. Note that each line of text highlights as the cursor moves to it.
3. Enter the EXECUTE key sequence. Note that the message "BLOCK PROTECTED" appears in the message area when the cursor is on a line in the protected area.

Module 39
RENUMBER

DESCRIPTION

The renumber function allows pages and paragraphs within a document to be renumbered. This accommodates the moving of pages and paragraphs from one location to another. In the case of pages, most document-oriented word processing systems automatically renumber pages when moving a page from one location to another. On some systems, however, new pages are inserted by giving them a decimal extension number.

For example, to insert a new page between existing pages 3 and 4, a GO TO PAGE 3.1 key sequence might be used. When this is done, the renumber function can be used to generate a new set of page numbers starting with the first page of the document as number 1. In the example above, the renumber function would change 3.1 to 4, page 4 would be renumbered as 5, and so on. The same principle can apply to paragraph renumbering.

APPLICATIONS

The renumber function can be used to reorder pages or numbered paragraphs within a document to ensure that they are in the proper sequence. If page 3 is switched to page 1 of a document, the renumber function can be used to change old page 3 to 1, old page 1 to 2, and old page 2 to 3. Many systems, however, do this automatically, thereby eliminating the need to use the renumber function to reassign page numbers.

TYPICAL OPERATION

In this illustration the renumber function will be used to change the page numbers of an existing five-page document consisting of pages 1, 2, 2.1, 2.2, and 3.

1. With a page of the five-page document displayed, press the RENUMBER key sequence.

2. Note that the renumber menu appears. Enter the beginning page number as 1, the ending page number as 5, and the starting page number as 1.

3. Press the EXECUTE key sequence and note that the page numbers are adjusted on the menu.

4. Return to the document by pressing the proper ESCAPE key sequence, and note that page 2.2 is now page 4.

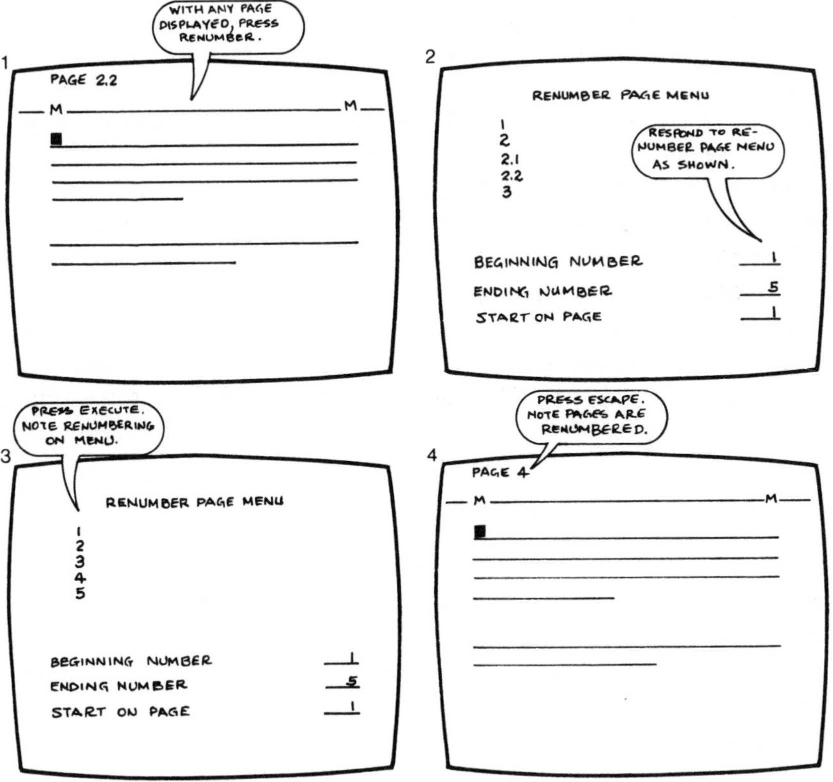

Module 40
HYPHENATION

DESCRIPTION

The hyphenation function is used to hyphenate words at the end of lines of text. This function is normally used to hyphenate text that has already been typed, although some systems allow hyphenation during text creation.

When the hyphenation function is activated, words that are normally wrapped to the beginning of the next line by the word wrap function can be hyphenated. Most systems highlight the characters in a word to be hyphenated and prompt the operator to select a hyphenation break point. The highlighted characters are commonly referred to as the *hyphenation zone.* Once the operator selects an appropriate breakpoint with the cursor and a HYPHENATE key sequence, a hyphen is inserted at the selected point and the balance of the word wraps to the beginning of the following line. If the word cannot be hyphenated, the operator has the option of wrapping the entire word without a hyphen. The hyphenation function often allows the selection of the text area size to be hyphenated. The operator may select a paragraph, a page, or an entire document.

Some systems have "hyphenation dictionaries," which make hyphenation decisions for the operator. Some dictionaries operate using rules of hyphenation; they are usually quite accurate, although the operator must occasionally override the results of a rule. Other systems use an actual hyphenation word list. This is a more accurate approach to hyphenation but requires more system storage.

APPLICATIONS

The automatic hyphenation function is used to make character spacing and line endings more uniform in appearance. Where hyphenation dictionaries exist within a system, the automatic hyphenation function saves the time necessary to look up words in a hyphenation reference book.

TYPICAL OPERATION

In this illustration a hyphenation function that involves operator decisions will be used to hyphenate line endings in an existing paragraph.

1. Move the cursor to the first character of the paragraph to be hyphenated and press the HYPHENATE key sequence. Note that the cursor automatically moves to the first word to be hyphenated (IMPORTANT) and the characters in the hyphenation zone I M P O R T A are highlighted.

2. Using the right arrow (East) key, move the cursor over the character A and press the EXECUTE key sequence.

3. Note that a hyphen appears after the T, the characters I M P O R T - move to the end of the preceding line, and A N T remains at the beginning of the line.

4. Note that the cursor automatically moves to the next word to be hyphenated. The procedure of step 2 is repeated for each word until all hyphenation decisions have been made. The system terminates the function automatically when all hyphenation decisions have been made for the selected text area.

Module 41
SPELLING DICTIONARY

DESCRIPTION

The spelling dictionary function is used to check the spelling of words in a document. Those systems that feature the spelling dictionary function have a stored list of correctly spelled words, which number from 20,000 to 100,000 words. When the function is activated, the words in the document being checked are compared with the words in the dictionary. When an unrecognized character string is encountered during the spelling check, the string is highlighted. The word processing system operator can check the word to verify that it is correct. If incorrect, the operator can correct it and move on to the next misspelled word.

Most spelling dictionaries allow new words to be added. When a new character string is encountered, the operator can enter it into the dictionary by pressing a special store key sequence.

Spelling dictionaries operate in three general ways. The first highlights misspelled words within the body of a document and prompts the operator to enter the correct spelling. The second gives the operator a list of misspelled words. Using the list, the operator may use the search and replace function to enter corrections. The third inserts a special symbol, or mark, by each misspelled word. The operator uses the search function to locate marked words and makes the necessary correction.

APPLICATIONS

The spelling dictionary function is used to check for misspelled words within a document. This function saves the time normally required to look up words in a regular dictionary, and it often catches spelling errors that would be completely overlooked without a spelling dictionary.

TYPICAL OPERATION

In this illustration the spelling dictionary function will be used to check the spelling on the page of a displayed document.

1. With the cursor at the left margin of the first line of text on a displayed document, enter the SPELLING DICTIONARY key sequence.

2. Note that the system highlights the first misspelled word (an unrecognized character string), and the prompt "CORRECT C, SKIP S, ADD A" appears in the screen message area.

3. Press *C*, enter the correct spelling, and press EXECUTE. The next misspelled word highlights, and the above prompt reappears.

4. This is a legitimate word; add it to the dictionary by pressing *A*. The spelling dictionary function terminates after the last misspelled word is found.

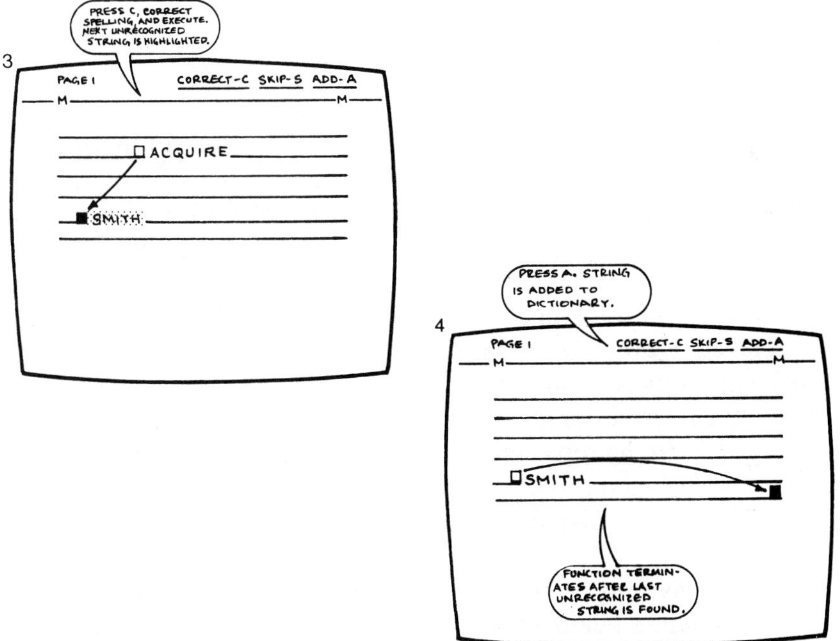

Module 42
AUTOMATIC TABLE OF CONTENTS

DESCRIPTION

The automatic table of contents function is used to reproduce designated document headings and page numbers in a list to comprise a table of contents, commonly referred to as "front matter." Those word processing systems that feature this function use special key sequences or symbols to identify the headings within a document. Once the headings are designated, a front-matter page is displayed. Next, a front-matter generation key sequence is entered, which causes the system to search and copy all designated headings. These headings are reproduced on the document's front-matter page, which can be reproduced when the document is printed. Some systems limit heading lengths. For example, the front matter may be limited to the first fifty characters.

Some systems can subordinate headings to several levels. For example, chapter heads may be centered, primary headings located at the left margin, secondary headings indented to the first tab, and so forth.

APPLICATIONS

The automatic table of contents function may be used to produce front matter for any document containing properly prepared chapter and paragraph headings.

TYPICAL OPERATION

In this illustration the automatic table of contents function will be used to compile all headings in a multiple-page document.

1. Create a document following the necessary paragraph heading conventions. In this example, a pound sign will be entered in the left margin in line with each paragraph heading.

2. Insert a new blank page 1 at the beginning of the document and prepare the table of contents heading. Old page 1 will become page 2.

3. Press the FRONT MATTER and EXECUTE key sequences. Note that each paragraph heading is listed with its page number.

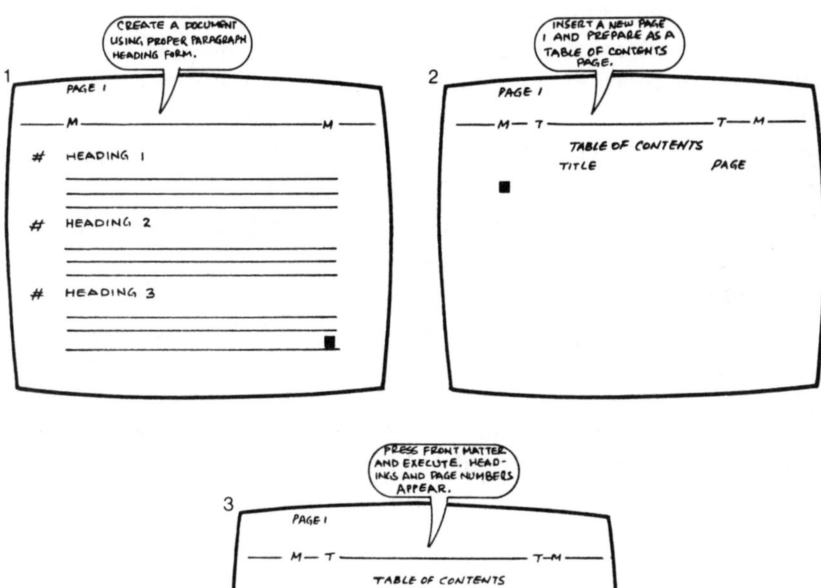

Module 43
LIST MERGE

DESCRIPTION

The list merge function is used to combine a list of variable information, such as names and addresses, with a corresponding base document. The base document, sometimes called a *mask*, is prepared so that blank spaces, called *fields*, exist to accommodate the variable information. The variables must be prepared in distinct sets, each set representing an individual document. Depending upon the system, the variables must either be arranged in the same sequence as they will appear in the base document or use a common field identification name. The base document and the list of variables are normally prepared as two separate documents.

Once the list and base letter documents are prepared, special LIST MERGE key sequences are entered. The system responds with either a set of prompts or a menu. These allow the operator to enter the document numbers to be merged and prepare for printing. When the printer is ready and the EXECUTE key sequence has been entered, a base letter is typed for each set of variables within the list.

APPLICATIONS

The list merge function is normally used to prepare form letters where names, addresses, salutations, and even words in the body of the letter vary from letter to letter. In addition to typing letters, the list merge function is used for addressing envelopes. A separate base letter can be prepared for the envelope and the same list used.

TYPICAL OPERATION

In this illustration the list merge function will be used to prepare three form letters. First, the base letter document will be prepared and filed. Next, a list document containing three sets of variables will be prepared and filed. Finally, the two documents will be merged using the list merge function.

1. Prepare the base letter with fields for title, first name and middle initial, last name, address, and city state zip. Note that the fields have specific names and are surrounded by merge symbols { }. File the base letter.

2. Prepare the list document ensuring that the list document variables are in the same order as the base document and that each variable is properly identified by the name at the top.

NOTE

Once the list document is filed, the LIST MERGE key sequence can be entered and a letter will be printed for each set of variables within the list document.

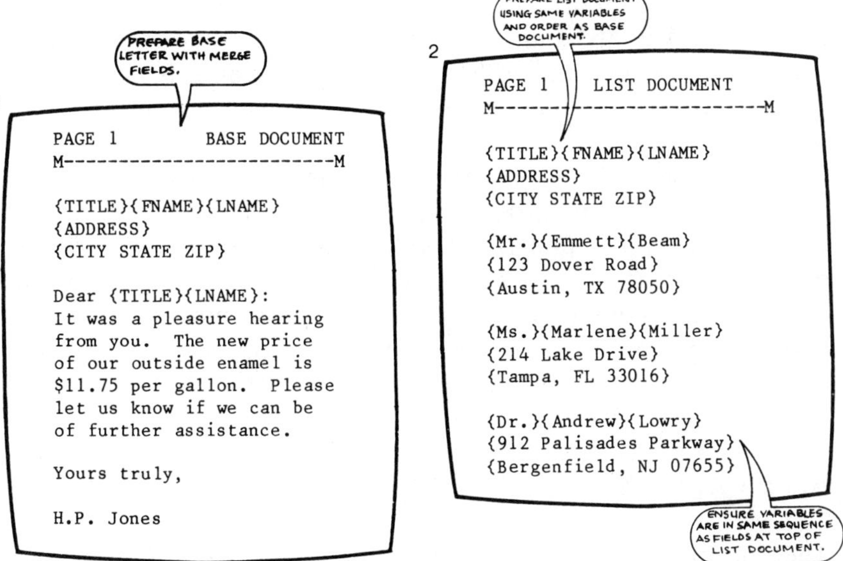

Module 44
DOCUMENT ASSEMBLY

DESCRIPTION

The document assembly function is used to combine separate documents into a single document. This function allows documents to be assembled in any sequence. Documents are assembled through either menus or prompts, where document numbers are specified in the desired order.

Documents are assembled into a new document, sometimes referred to as an "object document." Once the object document is opened, that is, the first blank page of the document is displayed and the format is set, the DOCUMENT ASSEMBLY key sequence is entered. On systems using menus, the document names or identification numbers are entered in the proper sequence. Once the menu is completed, the ASSEMBLY key sequence is entered and the documents are compiled in the new object document.

On those systems using prompts, documents are most often copied to the object document one at a time. This is sometimes referred to as "super copy" and is generally slower than a true document assembly function. However, super copy is not restricted to page or document boundaries. Any part of a document, such as a sentence, paragraph, or page, can be reproduced in the object document.

APPLICATIONS

The document assembly function is used to create new documents from a base of existing ones. For example, a legal document including several pages of Terms and Conditions can be created by assembling a group of contract clause documents.

TYPICAL OPERATION

In this illustration the document assembly function will be used to combine three existing documents into a new object document. A menu will be used to identify the documents.

1. With the first page of a new document displayed, press the DOCUMENT ASSEMBLY key sequence.

2. Note that a document assembly menu appears. Type the numbers of the documents to be assembled and press the EXECUTE key sequence.

3. Note that a copy of each document specified in the menu is assembled to form the object document.

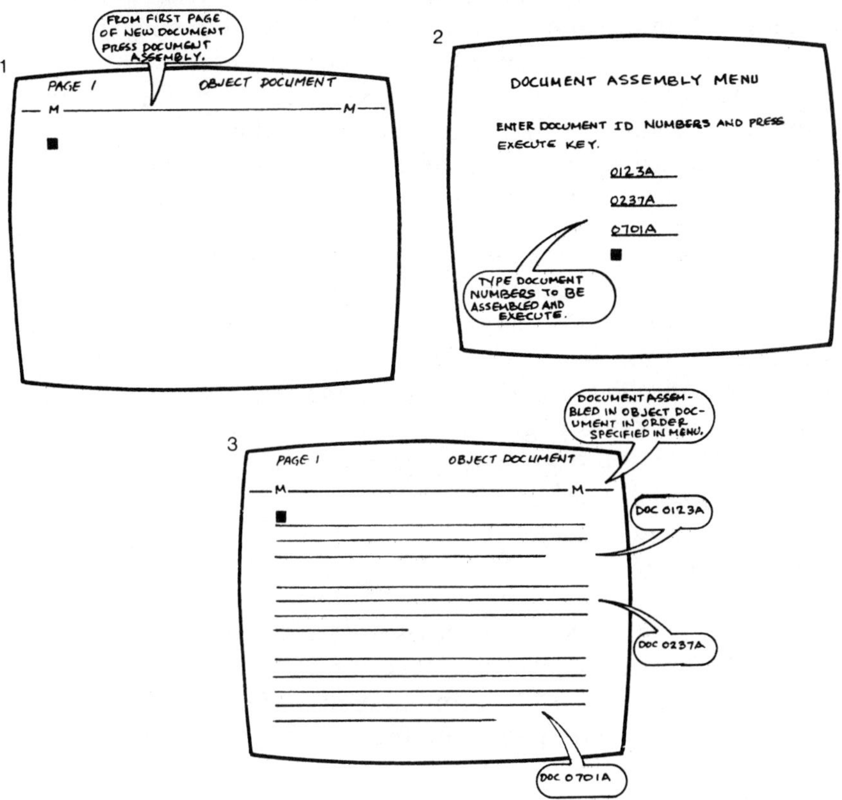

Module 45
HEADERS AND FOOTERS

DESCRIPTION

The headers and footers function is used to reproduce repetitive page heads and feet automatically, eliminating the need to type them on every page of a document. Page headers, which may contain such information as a chapter name, can be prepared on a special document header page. In like manner page footers, which may contain such information as a company name, document name, or page number, can be prepared on a special document footer page. Typically, header and footer pages are addressed either from a displayed document or from the print menu, prior to printing. When entered and activated, the headers and footers will be printed at the top and bottom of each page.

Many systems can automatically print page numbers in the header or footer area by inserting a special page symbol, such as {#}. This instructs the system to type the number of the page being printed within the braces. When inserting page numbers in a footer page, some systems allow right- and left-hand page numbering. The convention is for odd page numbers to be positioned at the bottom right-hand side of a page; even page numbers are positioned at the bottom left-hand side.

APPLICATIONS

The header and footer function is frequently used to reproduce running heads and feet on the pages of publications of all kinds, scripts, and tables. Headers and footers are also used on long memorandums where page numbering and common titles are required.

TYPICAL OPERATION

In this illustration the header function will be used to print a title and page number at the top of each page of a five-page document.

1. With the cursor located on a displayed document page, get the header page by entering the GO TO PAGE H key sequence.

2. With the header page displayed, type the title and page number key sequence {#}.

3. Press the ESCAPE key sequence and return to the displayed document.

NOTE

When the document is printed, the document title and page number will be automatically typed at the top of each page.

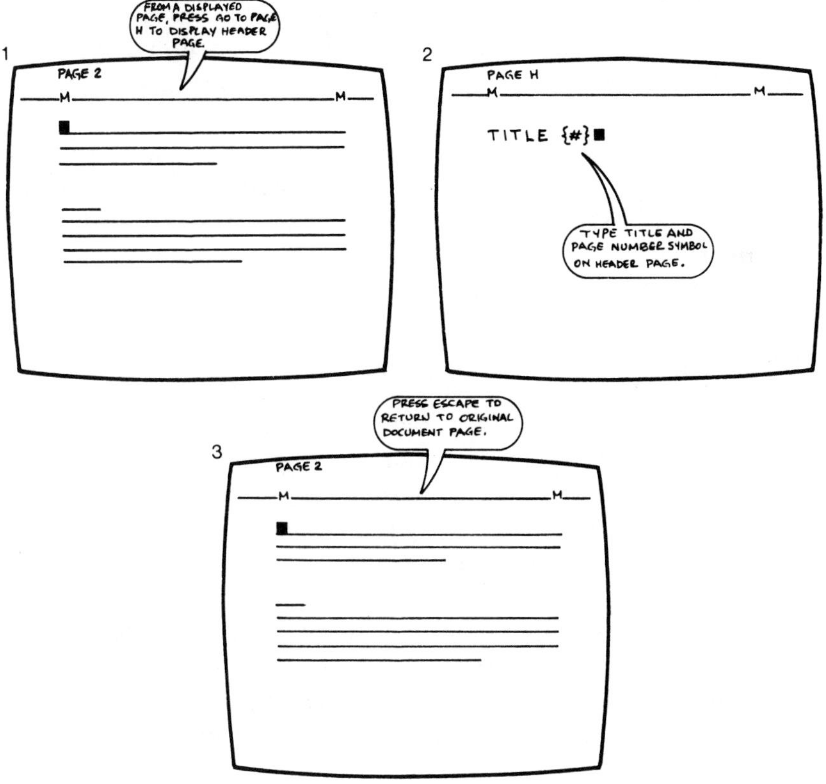

Module 46
AUTOMATIC RIGHT-HAND JUSTIFICATION

DESCRIPTION

The automatic right-hand justification function is used to align the right-hand margin of text vertically so that it will be straight. For example, if the right margin is set at character position 75, the last character of each line will be aligned with position 75. On some systems, the last character would be on 74 with a RETURN or automatic word-wrap character on 75. In either case, the end result is that the right-hand margin is automatically justified.

Justification is achieved by inserting full character spaces between words or smaller increments of space between characters within words. The insertion of extra space spreads each line of text to the margins. Character space between words can create "valleys" of white space on a page, which is undesirable. The insertion of small increments of space between characters is normally a preferred method.

The alternative to a justified right-hand margin is a "ragged" right-hand margin where each line ending may vary by several characters. Ragged right-hand margins are identical to text typed on a conventional typewriter where line endings simply fall wherever the RETURN key is pressed.

Some systems display right-hand justified text on the screen. When this is the case, a justification key sequence is entered while the document is displayed, and a system message or symbol appears to notify the operator that displayed text is justified.

Other word processing systems do not display right-hand justified text. On these systems justified or ragged right-hand margins are designated when the document is printed using the system's print menu.

APPLICATIONS

The automatic right-hand justification function is used to change the appearance of documents. It is particularly convenient when a multiple-column document, such as a newspaper, is prepared. This makes the "gutter," or white space between adjacent columns of text, smooth.

TYPICAL OPERATION

In this illustration the automatic right-hand justification function will be used to prepare a two-column page. The first column will be prepared on page 1 of the displayed document; the second column will be prepared on page 2. When the document is printed, column 1 and column 2 (page 1 and page 2) will be played out on the same sheet of paper.

1. With the cursor at the left margin of line 1 on the first page, move the cursor to the format line by pressing the FORMAT key sequence.

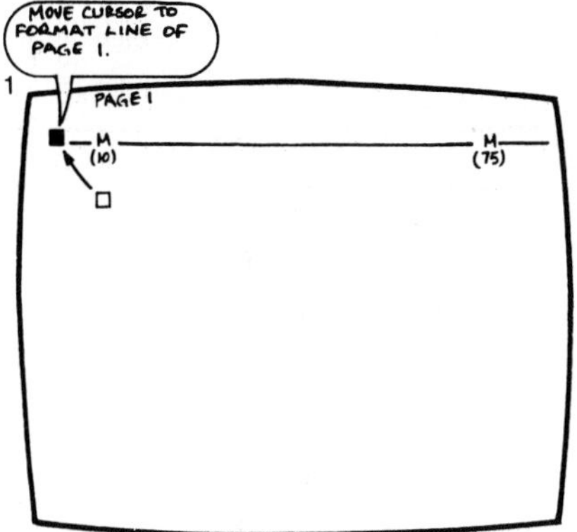

2. Set the left margin at character position 10, set the right margin at character position 40, and return the cursor to line 1 by pressing the EXECUTE key sequence.

3. Type the first column of text on page 1 ending on line 10.

4. Using the GO TO PAGE key sequence, get page 2; move the cursor to the format line by pressing the FORMAT key sequence.

5. Set the left margin at character position 45 and the right margin at character position 75, and return the cursor to line 1 by pressing the EXECUTE key sequence.

6. Type the second column of text on page 2 ending on line 10.

NOTE

This document will create two 30-character-wide columns of text separated by a straight 5-character-wide gutter of white space when it is printed. Page 1 will be printed first. Next, the sheet of paper can be manually rolled back to the first line, and page 2 will be printed.

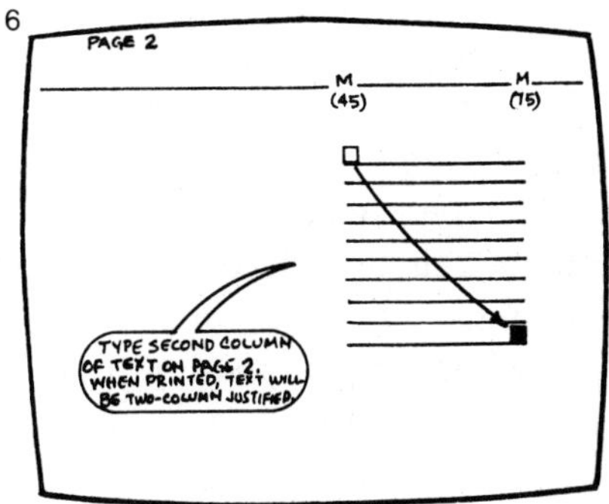

Module 47
PRINTING

DESCRIPTION

The printing function is used to select and print documents that have been created and filed on the word processing system. The print function sequence varies from system to system, although most have similar capabilities. Most systems allow concurrent printing, that is, one or more documents can be selected and printed while others are being displayed and edited. Some allow printing from a displayed document, while others require that documents to be printed be selected from a menu.

When the PRINT key sequence is entered, a print menu is displayed in which the operator selects such things as lines per page, characters per inch ("pitch"), number of copies, right-hand justification, and single-sheet or continuous-form paper feed. Some menus allow selection of margins and line spacing (single, space and one-half, double, etc.).

The standard line spacing is six lines per inch. Therefore a standard 8½-by-11-inch sheet of paper contains sixty-six lines from top to bottom. If an inch of space is to be left at the top and bottom of the printed sheet, the text area should occupy approximately fifty-four lines, leaving six blank lines above and below.

The most commonly used character spacing is 10- and 12-pitch, although 8-pitch is commonly used for presentation material that requires large characters. An inch of white space on either side of a standard sheet requires ten character spaces in 10-pitch, and twelve character spaces in 12-pitch. Ten-pitch margins can be located at character positions 10 and 75 for a 6½-inch-wide text area; 12-pitch margins can be located at character positions 12 and 90 to create the same text area.

Some systems can print in "proportional space," which gives each character a unit value. The lowercase *i* uses less space than the capital *W*, making the space between characters more uniform and, therefore, resulting in a more attractive document. Word processing system printers are generally of the daisy wheel or thimble type, described in Module 4 of this book.

When printing, it is important to align the paper carefully—both vertically and horizontally—to ensure straight, consistently registered text. The extra time used to verify proper alignment can save the time required to reprint a crooked page.

APPLICATIONS

The print function is used to output documents prepared on a word processing system. It is the "typewriter" of the system and allows the typing of any document that can be prepared on a standard office typewriter. A major advantage of a word processing system printer over a standard typewriter is that special print control characters can be imbedded in the text, such as bold print, stop code, double underscore, subscript, and superscript. Other word processing print function timesavers include such features as automatic word wrap, hyphenation, center, and indent.

TYPICAL OPERATION

In this illustration the print function will be used to type two copies of a standard document with margins set at character positions 10 and 75 on continuous-form paper.

1. With the first page of a two-page document displayed, press the PRINT key sequence to display the print menu.

2. With the print menu displayed, verify that all defaults are correct including sixty-six lines per page. Set the pitch at 10, copies at 2, and paper feed at *C* for "continuous."

3. Check to see that continuous-form paper is loaded and properly aligned in the printer and that the POWER switch is ON. Press the EXECUTE key sequence to begin printing.

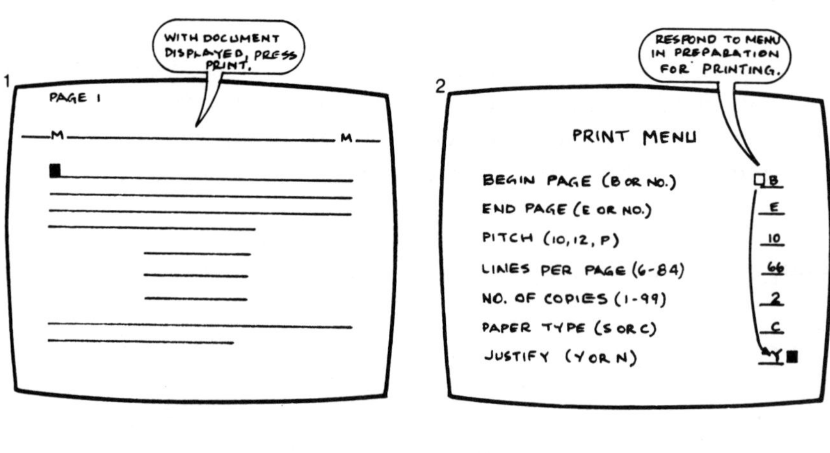

Module 48
PRINTER STOP CODE

DESCRIPTION

The printer stop code function is used to stop the printer at a specific point in a document. The stop code itself, which is produced by entering a special STOP CODE key sequence, is a special character or symbol that is typed, or imbedded, within the body of a document. Although the code can be viewed on the screen, it is never printed. It simply instructs, or "flags," the printer to stop printing at the stop code character position.

Once the printer stops, the word processing system operator may change the printer's type font or manually shift the paper. Then the printer can be restarted by pressing a prescribed key sequence or a RESTART switch on the printer, depending on the system being used.

APPLICATIONS

The stop code function is typically used to change type faces in a document. For example, an italic type face may be used to print a book's title or a ship's name. The stop code is entered in the document on either side of the title. When the printer stops at the first code, the operator changes the type face to italic and restarts the printer to type the title. When the printer stops at the second code, the operator changes back to the original-text type face and restarts the printer to continue printing standard text.

The stop code can also be used to type a form that uses nonstandard line spacing. By placing a stop code at the end of each line of text, the operator can manually align the form in the printer and restart it for proper line registration.

TYPICAL OPERATION

In this illustration the stop code function, represented by {S}, will be used to type a book title in italics.

1. With page 1 of a single-page document displayed, type the text to include the space in front of the book title.
2. Enter the STOP CODE key sequence, type the book title, enter the STOP CODE key sequence again, and finish typing the document.

NOTE

When the document is printed, the print wheel will be changed to italic to type the book title and changed back to the standard text face to finish printing the document.

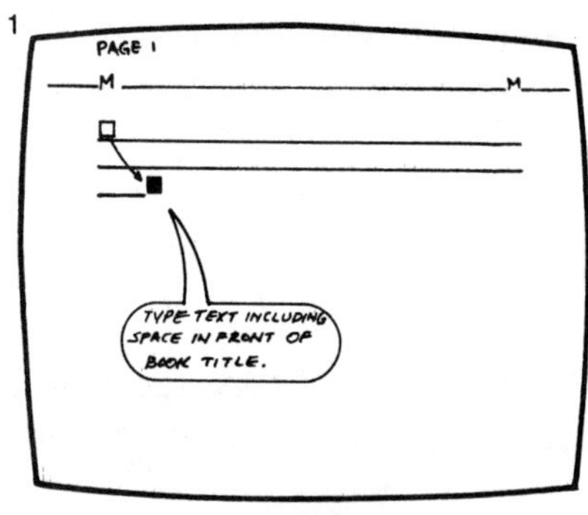

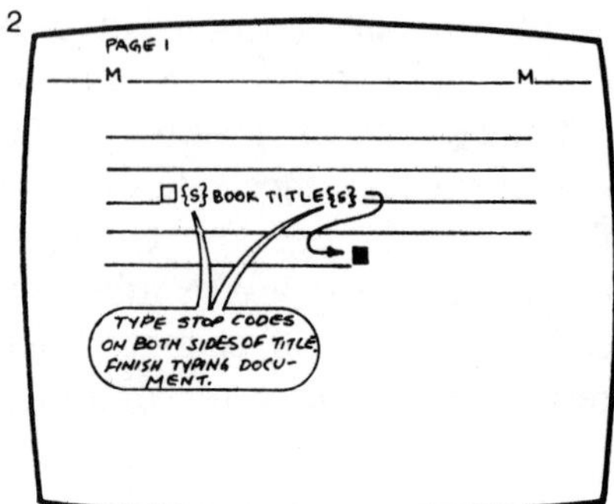

Module 49
AUTOMATIC UNDERSCORE AND DEUNDERSCORE

DESCRIPTION

The automatic underscore, sometimes called "autoscore," function is used to underline text. Some systems also feature automatic deunderscore, which erases the underscore located beneath blocks of text. These functions are not used by all word processing systems; those that feature autoscore have varied capabilities and use different approaches. When used, the automatic underscore function allows

1. Text to be underlined as it is being typed.
2. Areas of text to be underlined by defining the area's beginning and end points with the cursor in conjunction with a special key sequence.
3. Existing underlines to be removed from text areas by defining the area's beginning and end points with the cursor. This is the automatic deunderscore function.

The automatic underscore and deunderscore functions save keystrokes, making underlining or deunderlining text easier. Without the functions, the text would have to be typed first and then the area would be retraced with the underline key. Obviously, this requires double the number of keystrokes. When underlines are typed over with characters, the result is a strikeover. The character replaces the underline. Therefore the text characters must always be typed first and then underlined. Without the automatic deunderscore feature, the area to be deunderscored would require retyping to strike out the underlines.

Some word processing systems do not support underscores and characters on the same screen position. On these, an underline character is sometimes placed on the spaces prior to the first character and after the last character. To deunderscore, the beginning and end underline characters are simply deleted. This is a simple system and works well. The main disadvantage is that a "screen image" of underscored text isn't displayed.

APPLICATIONS

The automatic underscore function underlines text where underlines are required for such things as highlighting passages of text or following rules of English usage, as in designating book titles.

TYPICAL OPERATION

In this illustration the automatic underscore function will be activated to underline the book title in the sentence "THE BOOK TO READ IS *THE WORD PROCESSING HANDBOOK.*"

> **1.** Type the above sentence to the first character to be underscored.
>
> **2.** Press the AUTOSCORE key sequence and type the book title. Note that the text is automatically underlined as it is being typed.

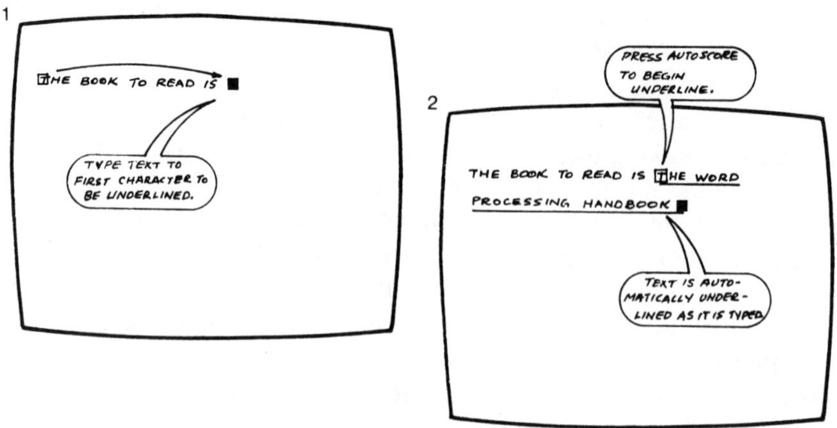

3. Press the AUTOSCORE key sequence again to terminate the function and type the ending period. Note that the period is not underlined.

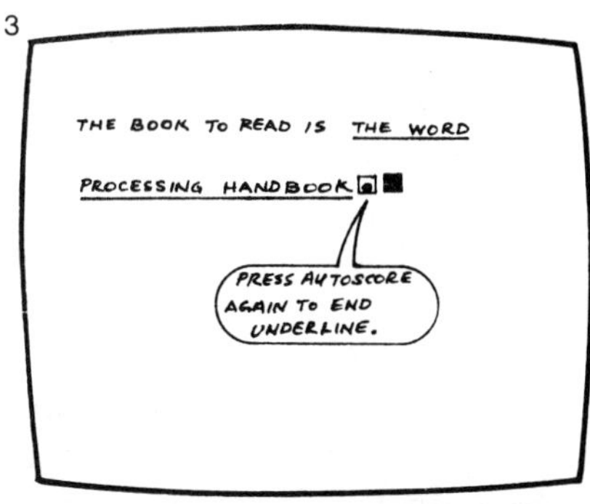

Module 50
DOUBLE UNDERSCORE

DESCRIPTION

The double underscore function often works in the same manner as the automatic underscore function. The double underscore places a double underline beneath the designated text instead of a single underline. As in the automatic underscore function, the beginning and end points of the double underscore must be defined. This is normally accomplished by placing the cursor over the first character to be double underlined and pressing the DOUBLE UNDERSCORE key sequence. Next, the text to be double underlined is typed. When the cursor is to the right of the last character to be double underlined, the DOUBLE UNDERSCORE key sequence is pressed again to terminate the function.

Some systems allow the double underscore function to be active during typing. On others, text may be double underscored by simply inserting the appropriate key sequence at the beginning and end points of the selected text.

APPLICATIONS

The double underscore function is normally used to highlight grand totals in financial reports. However, it is sometimes used for emphasis on certain passages of text differentiating from text that contains single underlines.

TYPICAL OPERATION

In this illustration the double underscore function will be used to underline the grand total at the bottom of a column containing three lines of numbers. We'll assume that the first two lines have already been typed and that the numbers on the second line have been underlined.

1. With the cursor at the beginning of line 3, type *T O T A L*, press the ALIGN TAB key sequence, and press the DOUBLE UNDERSCORE key sequence.
2. Type 1 0 . 5 0 and press the DOUBLE UNDERSCORE key sequence again to terminate the function.

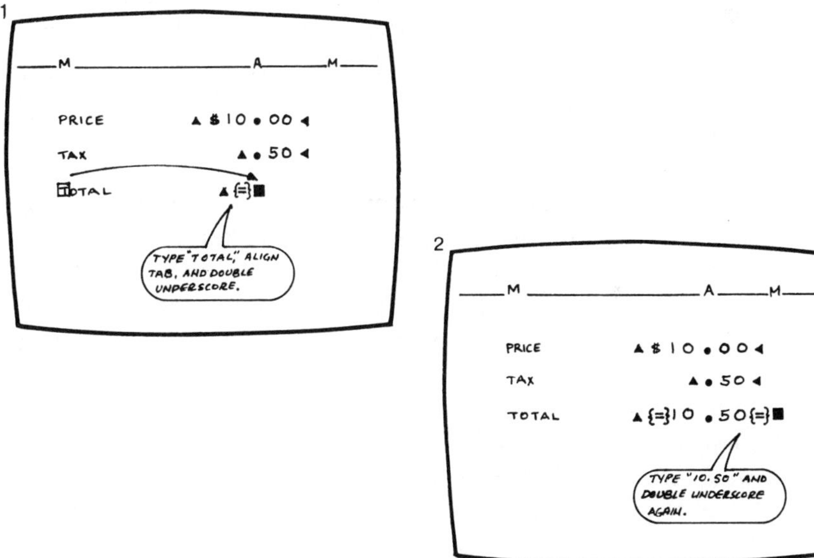

Module 51
BOLD PRINT (OR SHADOW PRINT)

DESCRIPTION

The bold print function, sometimes called "shadow print," is used to make selected text print darker, or bolder. This is accomplished by causing the printer to go into a multiple-strike mode when selected text is printed. Besides multiple strike, some printers shift a small amount to the left and right of the selected characters, making them thicker as well as darker.

The bold print code itself, which is produced by entering a special BOLD PRINT key sequence, is a special character or symbol that is typed, or imbedded, within the body of a document. Although the code can be viewed on the screen, it is never printed. It simply instructs, or "flags," the printer to bold print the specified text.

Bold printing is accomplished by simply entering the BOLD PRINT key sequence at the beginning and end points of the selected text. The words GRAND OPENING in the following sentence are an example of bold printing:

The **GRAND OPENING** is here at last!

APPLICATIONS

The bold print function is used for emphasis, making selected passages of text stand out in a document. It is sometimes used for chapter titles or paragraph headings, setting them aside from the rest of the text.

TYPICAL OPERATION

In this illustration the bold print function, represented by {B}, will be used to bold print some words in the body of a document.

1. With page 1 of a document displayed, type the text to include the space in front of the words to be bold printed.
2. Enter the BOLD PRINT key sequence, type the words, enter the BOLD PRINT key sequence again, and finish typing the document.

NOTE

When the document is printed, the selected text will be bold printed.

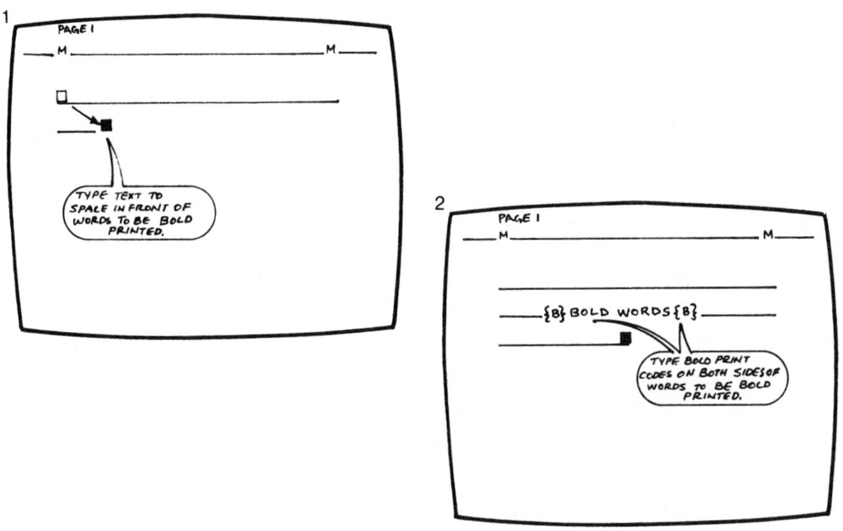

Module 52
SUBSCRIPT AND SUPERSCRIPT

DESCRIPTION

The subscript and superscript function allows selected characters to be printed a half-line space above or below the baseline, which is the imaginary line at the bottom of a line of text. Subscripts are printed below the base line; superscripts, above.

The subscript and superscript codes, which are produced by entering a special SUBSCRIPT or SUPERSCRIPT key sequence, are special characters or symbols that are typed, or imbedded, within the body of a document. Although the codes can be viewed on the screen, they are never printed. The codes simply instruct, or "flag," the printer to shift down or up a half-line space.

Printing subscripts or superscripts is accomplished by simply entering the appropriate SUBSCRIPT or SUPERSCRIPT key sequence at the beginning and end points of the selected text. One code causes the printer to roll up a half-line space; the other causes it to roll down. On most systems multiple entries of the subscript code cause the paper to roll up a half-line space each time the code is encountered. An equal number of superscript codes must be entered to return the paper to the original baseline. An example of a subscript and superscript is given in the following sentence:

Oxygen is O_2 and hydrogen is H^2O.

APPLICATIONS

The subscript and superscript functions are used to produce equations, footnote reference numbers, chemical notation (as shown above), and any other text where shifting a half-line up or down is desired.

TYPICAL OPERATION

In this illustration the subscript code, represented by {D}, and the superscript code, represented by {U}, will be used to print a subscript character in the body of a document.

> **1.** With page 1 of a document displayed, type the text to the position of the character to be subscripted.
>
> **2.** Enter the SUBSCRIPT key sequence {D}, type the character, enter the SUPERSCRIPT key sequence {U} to return following text to the original baseline, and finish typing the document.

NOTE

When the document is printed, the selected character will be located a half-line space below the baseline.

Module 53
OVERPRINT

DESCRIPTION

The overprint function is used to cause two characters to print over the same point of a printed document. When using the overprint function, the first character prints, the printer backspaces, and the second character overprints the first one. The overprint function allows the word processing system operator to select any two standard characters to be overprinted.

The overprint code itself, which is produced by entering a special OVERPRINT key sequence, is a special character or symbol that is typed, or embedded, within the body of a document. Although the code can be viewed on the screen, it is never printed. It simply instructs, or "flags," the printer to overprint the first selected character with the second.

Overprinting is accomplished by typing the first character, entering the OVERPRINT key sequence, and typing the second character to be overprinted. The zero (0) and slash sign (/) in the following sentence show how overprint looks when typed.

Capital oh is typed O; zero is typed Ø.

APPLICATIONS

The overprint function can be used to create special characters as in the example given above. The overprint function can also be used to strike through characters on systems that do not feature the strike through function, described in the next module.

TYPICAL OPERATION

In this illustration the overprint function, represented by {O}, will be used to overprint the "slash sign" character (/) with the hyphen character (–) in the body of a document.

1. With page 1 of a document displayed, type the text to include the first character (/) to be overprinted.

2. Enter the OVERPRINT key sequence, type the second character (–), and finish typing the document.

NOTE

When the document is printed, the "slash sign" (/) will be overprinted by the hyphen (–) to produce ∤ .

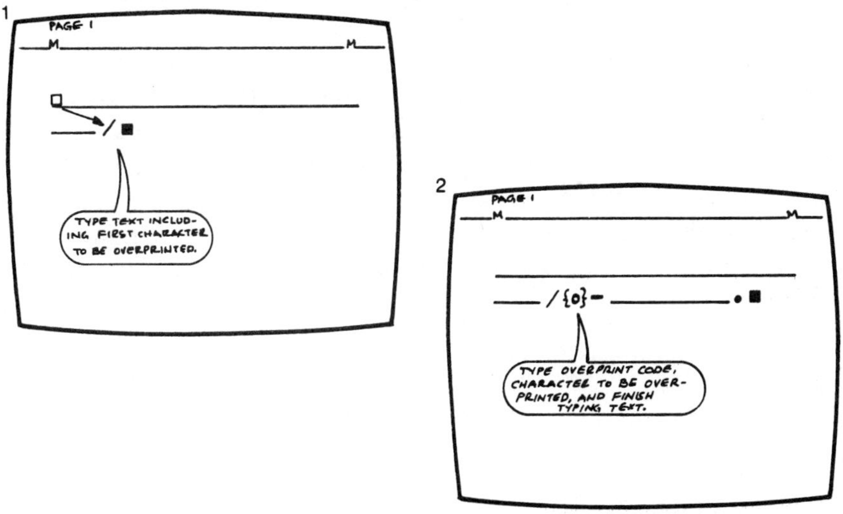

Module 54
STRIKE THROUGH

DESCRIPTION

The strike through function is used to strike over a specified character string within a document during printing. The text to be struck through is surrounded on each side by a special strike through code. The strike through code itself, which is produced by typing a special STRIKE THROUGH key sequence, is a special character or symbol that is typed, or imbedded, within the body of a document. Although the code can be viewed on the screen, it is never printed. It simply instructs, or "flags," the printer to type a specified strikeover character, which may be a hyphen, a slash sign, or an *X*, over all text and spaces located between the beginning and ending strike through codes. The strike through character is selectable on some systems, while others use a fixed character for strike through. Strike through was used on the word *green* in the following sentence:

> The quick red fox jumped over the lazy ~~green~~ brown dog.

APPLICATIONS

The strike through function is sometimes used to show words that have been deleted as a result of changes or editing. Words in the text can be shown struck through so that reviewers can determine what the document looked like before it was revised.

TYPICAL OPERATION

In this illustration the strike through function, represented by {-}, will be used to strike through some words in the body of a document.

> **1.** With page 1 of a document displayed, type the text to include the space in front of the words to be struck through.
>
> **2.** Enter the STRIKE THROUGH key sequence, type the words, enter the STRIKE THROUGH key sequence again, and finish typing the document.

NOTE

When the document is printed, the selected text will be struck through.

1

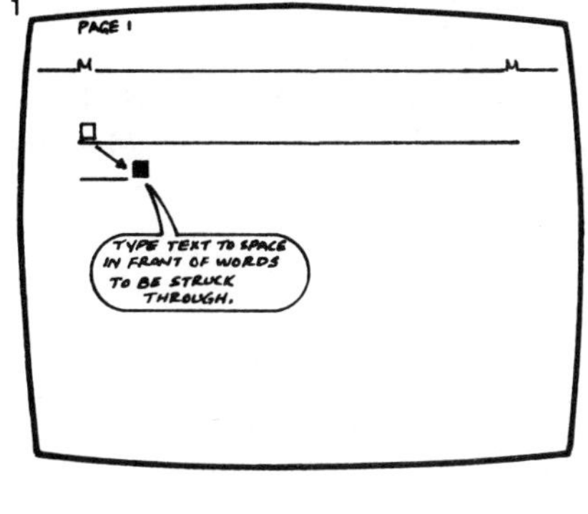

2

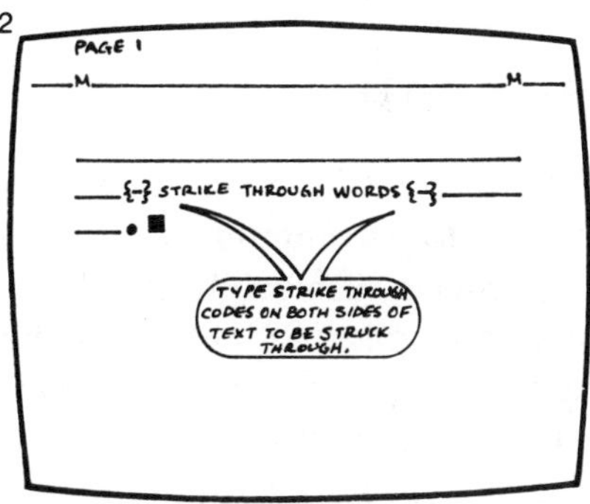

Module 55
NO PRINT

DESCRIPTION

The no print function causes a printer to enter an equivalent number of blank character spaces in place of a selected passage of text. Text to be no printed is surrounded on each side by a no print code. The no print code itself, which is produced by typing a special NO PRINT key sequence, is a special character or symbol that is typed, or imbedded, within the body of a document. Although the code can be viewed on the screen, it is never printed. It simply instructs, or "flags," the printer to leave blank space in place of the selected passage of text.

APPLICATIONS

The no print function is used to leave a fixed amount of blank space in text to accommodate later text entry. Once the first pass through a printer is achieved, the sheet can be realigned in the printer for a second pass. By changing the type font and no printing the text typed during the first pass, two different type styles can be entered on the same sheet with relative ease. An alternative to this is to use stop codes each time a type-font change is required. However, this can be very time consuming when a half-dozen or more font changes are needed.

TYPICAL OPERATION

In this illustration the no print function, represented by {N}, will be used to no print a passage in the body of a document.

1. With page 1 of a document displayed, type the text to include the space in front of the text passage to be no printed.
2. Enter the NO PRINT code, type the text passage, enter the NO PRINT code again, and finish typing the document.

NOTE

When the document is printed, the selected text will be no printed.

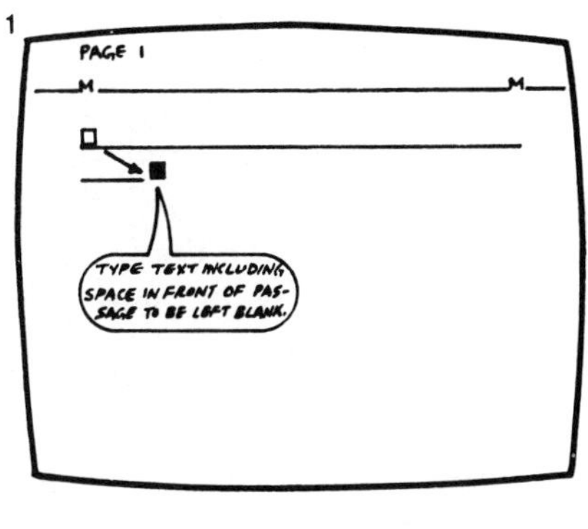

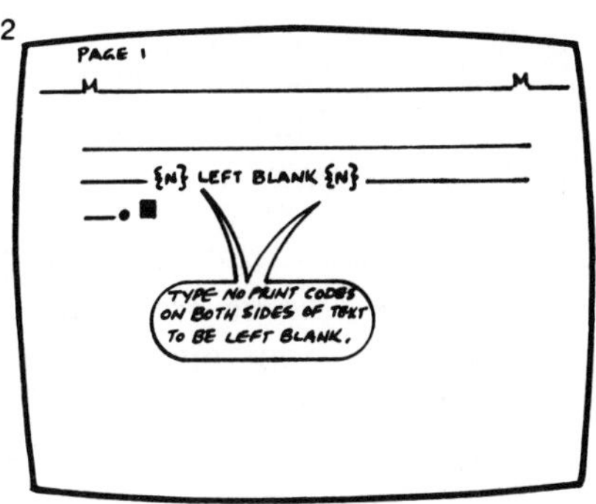

Module 56

PRINTING SPECIAL CHARACTERS AND SYMBOLS

DESCRIPTION

Many word processing systems allow the printing of special characters and symbols, such as Greek characters and math symbols. Some systems display special characters on the screen and offer printer type fonts containing a matching character set. Other systems use substitute key sequences to represent the symbols on the screen, supplying reference books or quick reference cards to help the operator determine what key sequence to use to print out a special character or symbol.

Special character type fonts can be obtained on many printers. When a printer has a single print head, which is most common, the special-character type font must be installed on the printer to reproduce special characters and symbols. There are also dual-head printers, sometimes called "twin track" printers, that automatically use the print head required to reproduce the specified character. These save time where special characters and symbols are frequently used.

When entering special symbols code key in text, the key sequence sometimes includes a special CONTROL or ESCAPE key in combination with a standard text character or number. This is often referred to as "supershift," as opposed to pressing a standard shift key sequence to type an uppercase character.

APPLICATIONS

Special characters or symbols are used to type mathematical and technical documents. Greek characters and math symbols are used extensively in the preparation of equations and formulas.

TYPICAL OPERATION

In this illustration the Yen symbol code, represented by {Y}, will be entered in the body of a document.

1. With page 1 of a document displayed, type the text to the space where the Yen symbol character will be typed.
2. Enter the Yen symbol code {Y} and finish typing the document.

NOTE

When the document is printed, the Yen symbol will be printed at the selected point.

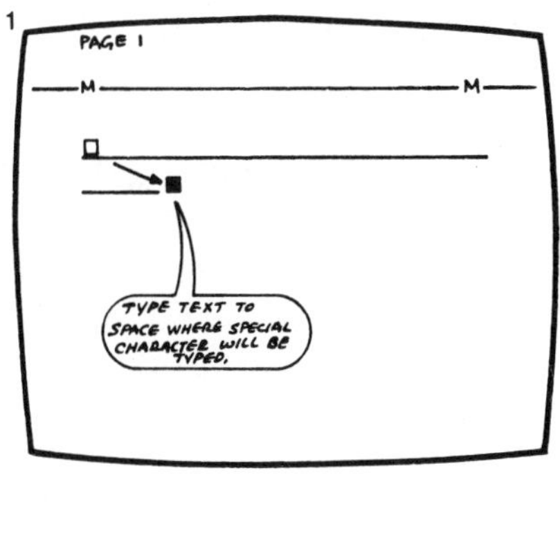

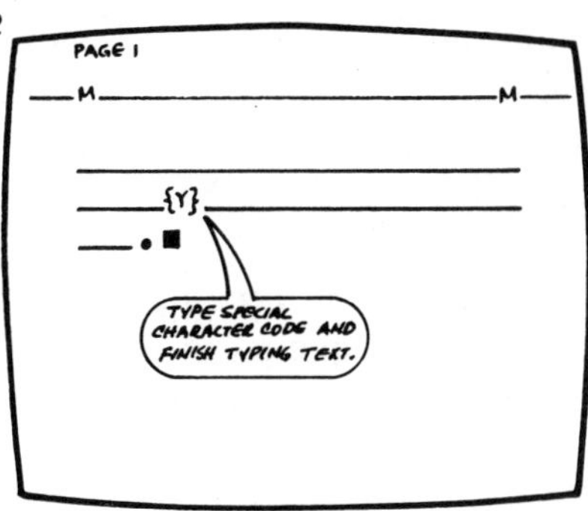

Module 57
REVERSE ROLL (OR TOP OF FORM)

DESCRIPTION

The reverse roll function, sometimes called "top of form," is used to reverse the direction of printer line feed. When used, the page being printed reverses direction, returning to the first line of the printed page.

The reverse roll code itself, which is produced by entering a special REVERSE ROLL key sequence, is a special character or symbol that is typed, or imbedded, within the body of a document. Although the code can be viewed on the screen, it is never printed. It simply instructs, or "flags," the printer to reverse direction to the top of the page.

Reverse roll is accomplished by simply entering the REVERSE ROLL key sequence at the point in the document where the operator wishes the sheet being printed to return to the first line.

APPLICATIONS

The reverse roll function is used to print multiple-column text on a single sheet of paper. When producing a two-column page, the reverse roll function types the first column, automatically returns the sheet of paper to the first line, and types the second column of text. In the alternative to reverse roll, the operator would stop the printer at the end of the first column, manually reverse roll the sheet of paper to the first line, and then restart the printer to type the second column.

Reverse roll can also be used to type two or more type faces on a single sheet. For example, a document can be prepared in two sections where all text using one face is typed in one section, and all text using the second face is typed in another. Each section leaves blank spaces or uses the no print function where the other face is to be typed. A reverse roll code and stop code are imbedded at the bottom of the first section to return the sheet to the first line and stop printing. The type font is then changed and a second pass is made, filling in the blank spaces with the second type face.

TYPICAL OPERATION

In this illustration the reverse roll code, designated by {R}, will be used to prepare a two-column page. The first column, which will end with a reverse roll code, will be prepared with margins set at character positions 10 and 40. The second column will be prepared with margins set at character positions 45 and 75.

1. With the cursor at the left margin of line 1 on the first page, move the cursor to the format line by pressing the FORMAT key sequence.

2. Set the left margin at character position 10, set the right margin at character position 40, and return the cursor to line 1 by pressing the EXECUTE key sequence.

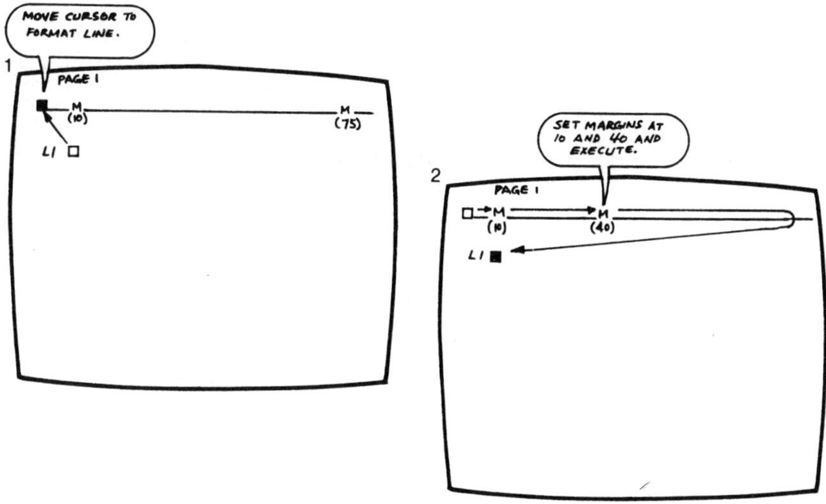

3. Type the first column of text on page 1 ending line 10 with a RETURN, a REVERSE ROLL code {R} and RETURN on line 11, and the cursor on line 12.

4. Move the cursor to the format line by pressing the FORMAT key sequence.

5. Set the left margin at character position 45 and the right margin at character position 75, and return the cursor to line 12 by pressing the EXECUTE key sequence.

6. Type the second column of text ending line 21 with a RETURN.

NOTE

This document will create two 30-character-wide columns of text separated by a 5-character-wide gutter of white space when it is printed. Column 1 will be printed first, the sheet of paper will be rolled back to the first line, and column 2 will be printed.

Module 58
TYPE THROUGH (OR TYPEWRITER MODE)

DESCRIPTION

The type through function, sometimes called "typewriter mode," is featured on some word processing systems to allow a word processing operator to use the system like a standard typewriter. As keys are pressed on the system's keyboard, corresponding characters are typed by the printer.

This function is activated by pressing a special TYPE THROUGH key sequence. Sometimes this is done when a document is displayed on the screen, or it may be done from a system menu. Often, the display screen "echoes" the characters being typed to enable the operator to see the text as it is being entered.

APPLICATIONS

Type through is used to prepare such things as envelopes and small labels where creating, filing, and printing would be more time consuming than simply typing them. This function makes a word processing system a true typewriter replacement. Systems that do not feature this function often require users to have access to standard typewriters for preparing small notes and labels.

TYPICAL OPERATION

In this illustration the type through function will be used to address an envelope.

1. With a document displayed, enter the TYPE THROUGH key sequence, designated by {T}.

2. Insert an envelope in the printer and type the address as on a standard typewriter.

3. Note that typed characters are also displayed on the screen. Terminate the type through function by entering the TYPE THROUGH key sequence {T} a second time.

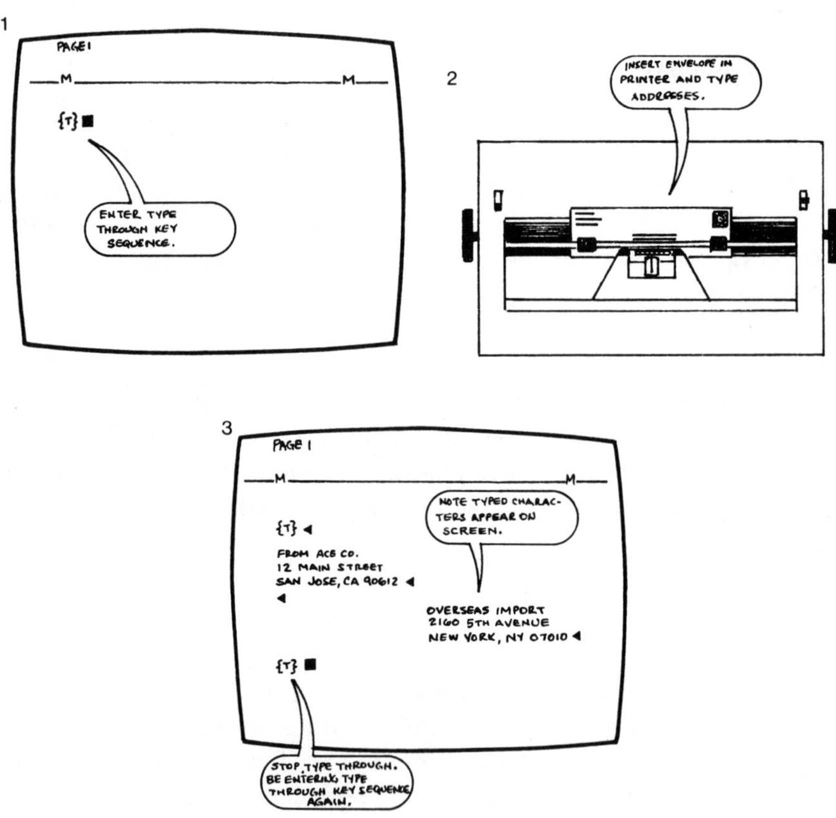

Module 59
GLOSSARY
(OR USER-DEFINED KEYS)

DESCRIPTION

The glossary, or user-defined keys, function allows the word processing system operator to save frequently used key sequences and recall them for use as needed. The mechanics involved in saving and recalling frequently used keystrokes varies from system to system. Some systems require the use of a special user-defined key menu, in which keystrokes are entered, labeled, and stored. To recall the keystrokes, the cursor is positioned over the point in the document where they are to appear, a special RECALL key sequence is entered, and the saved keystrokes automatically appear beginning at the cursor position.

Other systems allow the creation of special glossary documents that contain a number of addressable keystroke sequences. Each sequence is given a label, such as A or B1. Once a glossary document is created and stored, it may be addressed from a displayed document. When the glossary is "called," the desired keystroke sequence can be recalled by positioning the cursor and entering the keystroke label, such as GLOSSARY R. The stored keystroke sequence will appear, beginning at the cursor position.

APPLICATIONS

The glossary, or user-defined keys, function is used to save the time required to type frequently used key sequences or passages of text. For example, if a company name is used over and over in the course of a day, the name may be recalled with the glossary function by typing two keystrokes, such as GLOSSARY A, instead of thirty-seven keystrokes, such as THE PERSONNEL PLACEMENT COMPANY, INC.

TYPICAL OPERATION

In this illustration the glossary function will be used to recall a stored key sequence.

> **1.** During normal document text creation, the cursor reaches a position in the document where a glossary keystroke sequence can be recalled to save typing time.
>
> **2.** Attach the glossary to the document by entering the GLOSSARY key sequence and identifying glossary number. Note the prompt "GLOSSARY ATTACHED."
>
> **3.** Recall the stored keystroke sequence by entering the GLOSSARY key sequence and the keystroke sequence label. Note that the keystroke sequence appears beginning at the cursor position.

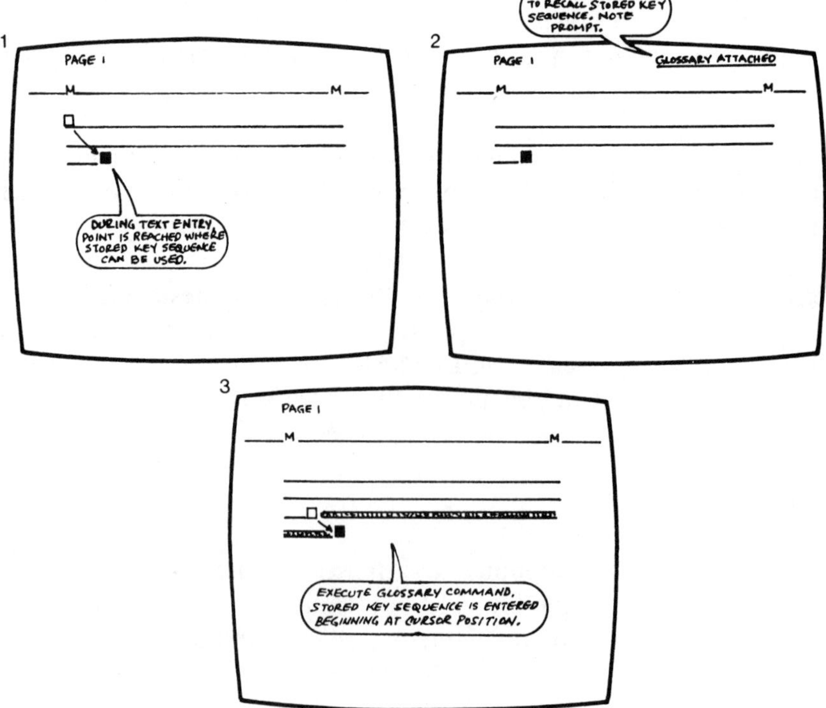

Module 60
MATHEMATICAL FUNCTION

DESCRIPTION

The mathematical function, sometimes called "mathpak," is used to add and subtract columns and rows of numbers. Many word processing systems also perform multiplication and division. Each system's mathematical function follows set rules, requiring that all numbers to be computed be located on align tabs. The math document itself must often be prepared by using special formats.

Some systems use equations where columns and rows of numbers are assigned location coordinates. A four-row, four-column table of numbers may be given the following coordinates:

	C1	C2	C3	C4
R1	3	5	7	15
R2	2	12	11	25
R3	21	6	1	28
R4	26	23	19	68

Note that column 4 and row 4 are total columns. The equation written to add the first three numbers of the first row and place the results in the row 1 column 4 position would be

$$R1C4 = R1C1 + \mathrm{R}1C2 + R1C3$$

Equations to find the totals of other rows and columns would be written in a similar manner. Symbols, called operators, used for subtraction, multiplication, and division are typically -, *, and /.

For example, to place the results of dividing row 1 column 1 by row 2 column 3 at row 2 column 4, the equation would be

$$R2C4 = R1C1/R2C3$$

Multiplying the above equation by 3.5 would be written

$$R2C4 = 3.5 * (R1C1/R2C3)$$

Trailing or leading minus signs (-) or parentheses are commonly used to designate negative numbers when using the mathematical function.

To execute the equation, the cursor is often positioned on the equation and a special MATH key sequence is entered. The results are automatically entered in the specified row and column coordinate.

Other systems perform addition and subtraction of columns and rows by simply placing the cursor at the first character of the column or row and pressing an appropriate key sequence, such as *R*+ to add the row. In this case, a blank field must be provided at the end of the row where the result will be entered.

APPLICATIONS

The mathematical function is frequently used to prepare financial documents. Once numbers are entered in the document, the answers can be computed by the system by activating the mathematical function. This saves operator time and ensures accurate answers.

TYPICAL OPERATION

In this illustration the mathematical function will be used to add four numbers in a column. The result will be placed on the fifth line, beneath the column of numbers.

1. With a document containing a vertical column of four numbers set on an align tab, move the cursor to the first digit of the first number.

2. Press the ADD key sequence; note that the results appear on the fifth line.

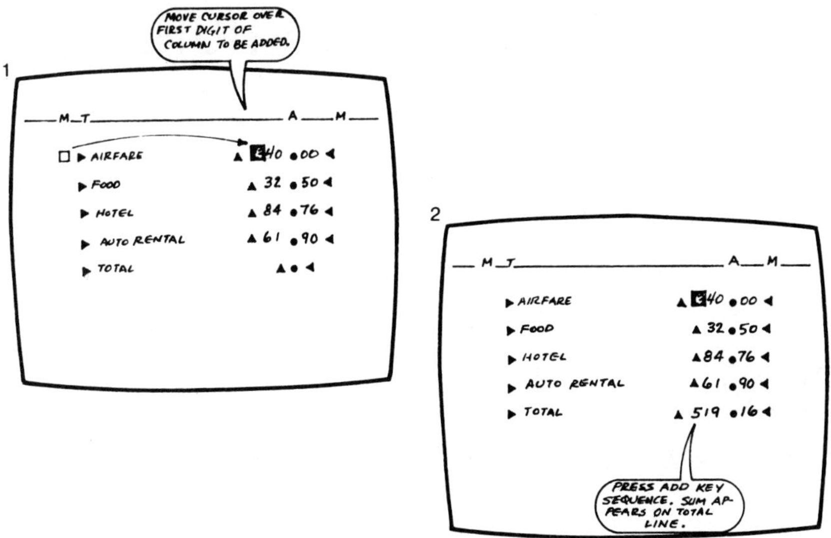

Module 61
TELECOMMUNICATIONS

DESCRIPTION

The telecommunications function allows word processing systems to communicate document files with other word processing or data processing systems. The communications function requires

1. Communications software
2. Communications hardware
3. Telephone system connection device (modem or acoustic coupler)
4. A system with which to communicate, having compatible software, hardware, and telephone system connection
5. Qualified word processing system operators

The communications software provides communications menus, in which communication speeds, protocols (a specific communications code), and sending or receiving document numbers can be identified. Communications hardware includes the physical equipment within the word processing system used to convert outgoing files to a data form suitable for transmission and incoming data to a form suitable for filing within the system. The telephone system connection equipment is necessary to couple the word processing system to the telephone system.

Of course, a compatible system with which to communicate must be available. Finally, an operator qualified to send and receive filed documents is necessary.

APPLICATIONS

The telecommunications function is used to send documents from one location to another, saving the time required to use ordinary mail. In fact, telecommunications is referred to as "electronic mail." Telecommunications can also tie word processing systems to other devices that use compatible speeds and protocols. For example, files can be transferred from word processing systems to data processing and typesetting systems by using telecommunications.

TYPICAL OPERATION

In this illustration the telecommunications will be used to send a filed document from one word processing system to another.

1. With the main menu displayed, select the telecommunications function by moving the cursor to telecommunications and pressing the EXECUTE key sequence. Note that the telecommunications menu appears.

2. With the telecommunications menu displayed, select teletype communications by moving the cursor to TTY and pressing the EXECUTE key sequence. Note that the TTY menu appears.

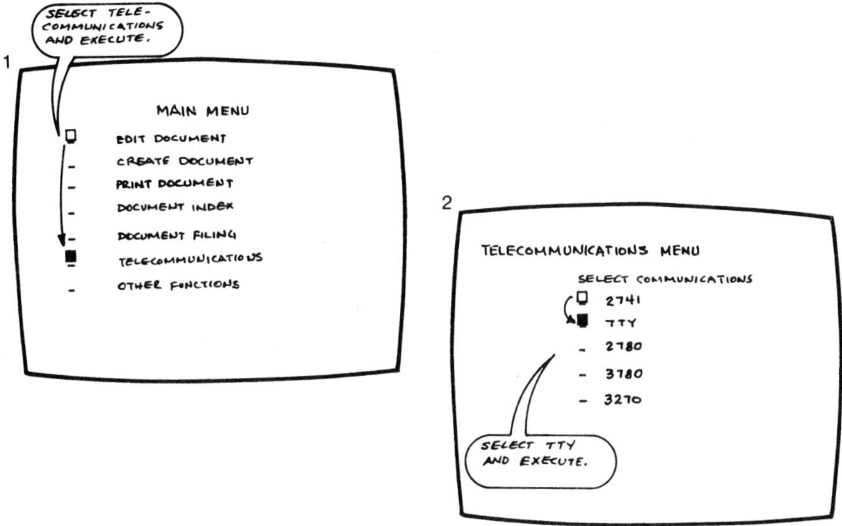

3. With the TTY menu displayed, verify that BAUD is set to 300, and PARITY is set to *E* (for EVEN). Enter the document ID number to send, and note the prompt "DATA SET NOT READY."

4. Pick up the phone, dial the telephone number of the receiving system, and listen for a high-pitched carrier tone. Upon receipt of the tone, place the telephone handset in the acoustic coupler. Note that prompt changes to "DATA SET READY."

5. Press the EXECUTE key sequence, and watch the selected document move across the screen as it is being transmitted.

6. Upon completion, press the ESCAPE key sequence and hang up the telephone.

APPENDIX
WORD PROCESSING SYSTEM EXERCISES

1. *Introduction*

a. Draw and give the meaning of five symbols used in word processing illustrations.
b. What term is used to define the intersection of line 15 and character 25 on a display screen?
c. Name three types of magnetic storage media.
d. What is the name of the key sequence frequently used to complete a word processing function?

2. *Display-Based Word Processing System Categories*

a. Write the names of three categories of display-based word processing systems.
b. In which category of a word processing system would a standard office typewriter belong?
c. What is used to visualize text on non-display-based word processing systems?
d. What is the purpose of a storage device?

3. *Word Processing System Work Stations*

a. Name the two major parts of a display-based word processing system work station.
b. Name three types of display screens.

c. Compute the screen load of a 58-line by 98-character display.
d. Describe the difference between a *code-key* and a *mnemonic keyboard system.*

4. Common Word Processing System Printing Devices

a. List three common types of letter-quality printers.
b. Name two printers commonly used in data processing.
c. Describe a daisy wheel.
d. Which types of printer commonly use chains of characters?

5. Paper Feed Devices

a. Name two paper feed devices.
b. What is the major advantage of paper feed devices?
c. Which types of printer are frequently restricted to continuous-form paper?
d. Which type of paper feed device uses feed pins?

6. Storage Devices and Media

a. Write a physical description of diskettes and disks.
b. Name three ways in which magnetic storage devices can be damaged.
c. What kind of pen should be used when writing on the jacket of a magnetic diskette?
d. What is the value of backing up magnetic media?

7. Turning the Equipment On and Off

a. What kind of power source is often required by word processing systems?

b. What document should be carefully read prior to turning word processing system power on and off?

c. What can happen to documents stored on magnetic media if they are improperly inserted or removed, or if power is improperly turned on or off?

8. *Cursor Control*

a. Give another name used to describe the cursor.

b. List the keys commonly used to move the cursor.

c. What other names are commonly used to describe the up, down, left, and right arrow keys?

d. What two keys can be used to move the cursor down to the next line of the display screen?

9. *Word Processing System Prompts*

a. Where can system prompts be seen?

b. What are the two general types of prompts?

c. How can prompts help an operator perform a word processing function?

d. Which type of prompt tells an operator that the system is busy performing a certain task?

10. *Menus*

a. Describe how menus are used.

b. What is the difference between a *main menu* and a *submenu?*

c. What is a *default value*?

d. How can a print menu be used to change an existing value of 12-pitch printing to 10-pitch printing?

11. Document Filing and Retrieval

a. What term is used to describe the act of saving a document on a word processing system's storage device?
b. What term is used to describe the act of recalling a document from a word processing system's storage device?
c. What is an important factor to consider when evaluating word processing systems?
d. How are menus used on some systems to assist in recalling a stored document?

12. Screen Graphics

a. What is the purpose of screen graphics?
b. What is an advantage to being able to suppress screen graphics?
c. Draw the symbols for TAB and RETURN.
d. How many blank lines of text are indicated by three successive RETURN symbols where the first RETURN symbol is at the end of a line of text?

13. Return (Carriage Return)

a. What other labels are sometimes engraved on the RETURN key?
b. Describe two uses for the RETURN key.
c. After pressing the RETURN key at the end of a line of text, where will the cursor be located?
d. What is a destructive RETURN?

14. Automatic Word Wrap

a. Describe the automatic word wrap function.

b. When a word is too long to fit on a line, where does it go when the automatic word wrap function is active?
c. How does the automatic word wrap function make the word processing operator more productive?
d. Which keystroke is eliminated by the automatic word wrap function?

15. Screen Status Lines

a. Where are screen status lines normally found on display-based word processing systems?
b. Name three pieces of information that are typically found in screen status lines.
c. What is indicated by the letters *J* and *H* in a screen status line?
d. What changes in the screen status line when the cursor is moved from line 3, character position 10 to line 15, character position 20?

16. Format

a. What three common document dimensions are shown on the format line?
b. Where is the cursor positioned when setting a document format?
c. How can existing tabs and margins be erased on a format line?
d. How is the cursor returned from the format line to the text area?

17. Tab (Standard)

a. Where can tab positions normally be viewed?
b. How is the cursor advanced to a tab position on a display-based word processing system?

c. Name two applications using the standard tab.

d. Describe how tabs are normally set on word processing systems.

18. Align Tab (or Decimal Tab)

a. Which character is normally vertically aligned when using the align tab function?

b. What is a *combination tab*?

c. When typing numbers on an align tab, in which direction does the text move prior to typing the align character?

d. What kinds of documents are ideally suited for the align tab function?

19. Outline Tab

a. What is the primary purpose of the outline tab relative to the beginning of new lines of text?

b. If *T* is used to designate a standard tab, what symbol might be used to designate an outline tab?

c. What key is normally pressed to advance the cursor to the outline tab position?

d. Describe a typical application of the outline tab function.

20. Tabular Editing

a. How do word processing systems commonly manipulate text?

b. How do tabular editing functions differ from common editing functions?

c. What is meant by a *one-tab column shift*?

d. Describe an application of the tabular editing function.

21. Flush Right (Using Align Tab)

a. If flush right is a secondary purpose of the align tab, what is the primary purpose?
b. Describe how the right-hand edge of text can be made smooth by using the align tab.
c. When line lengths vary, describe the left-hand margin of text.
d. What key is typically pressed to terminate each line of text when performing the flush right function?

22. Reformat

a. List three format items that can be changed by using the reformat function.
b. How is text to be reformatted usually identified?
c. What must be done with the cursor when resetting document format?
d. Describe a use of the reformat function.

23. Strikeover

a. Compare the word processing strikeover function with performing a strikeover on a standard office typewriter.
b. How is the cursor used in conjunction with the strikeover function?
c. What characters can be struck over by using the strikeover function?
d. Is blanking out a word by using the space bar an example of strikeover? Explain.

24. Delete

a. What is another word for *delete*?
b. Describe what is meant by text *close up*.

c. List five things that can be eliminated by using the delete function.
d. How is the text to be deleted defined?

25. *Insert*

a. What is another word for *insert*?
b. If an insert is made in the middle of a sentence, what happens to the following text?
c. If a new page is inserted between existing pages 1 and 2, list the new page numbers by using a standard page renumbering system and using extension numbers.
d. List five things that can be inserted within a document.

26. *Move*

a. Describe the move function in your own words.
b. Describe an application of the move function.
c. When text is reinserted in a document when using the move function, what happens to the text immediately following the moved material?
d. What other word processing functions could be used as a substitute for the move function?

27. *Copy (or Duplicate)*

a. Describe the copy function in your own words.
b. Think of and describe an application for the copy function.
c. How is the text to be copied selected?
d. What other word processing functions could be used as a substitute for the copy function?

28. Center

a. Where does line-centered text appear relative to the left and right margins of a document?
b. What is meant by *centering over a selected point*?
c. Describe two applications of the center function.
d. Without the center function, how would text be centered on a line?

29. Indent

a. How does the indent function differ from the tab function?
b. Describe a typical application of the indent function.
c. How is the indent function typically canceled?
d. Without the indent function, how could the space bar be used to indent text?

30. Scrolling (Horizontal and Vertical)

a. Describe what happens to text when it is scrolled.
b. What is the difference between *smooth scrolling* and *incremental scrolling*?
c. What is an application of horizontal scrolling?
d. How can an operator view a fifty-line page on a twenty-two-line display screen?

31. Go to Page, Get

a. What effect does the go to page function have on the cursor?
b. What key would be included in the GO TO PAGE key sequence to display page 3 of a document?
c. How would an arrow key be used in conjunction with the GO TO PAGE key sequence?

d. With the cursor at the top of a displayed page, how could the cursor be moved to the bottom of the page without using the go to page function?

32. *Note (or Return to a Specified Position)*

a. Describe the purpose of the note function in your own words.

b. What is meant by a *reference mark*?

c. What is an alternative to using the note function?

d. What other function key sequence is commonly used with the note function?

33. *Search (or Find)*

a. What is a *character string?*

b. How is a character string used in conjunction with the search function?

c. Describe how a search area is identified.

d. What is meant by *global search*?

34. *Replace*

a. Describe the purpose of the replace function.

b. How are prompts and menus used with the replace function?

c. Because the replace function replaces specific character strings with others, how could you prevent replacing the character string T H E in the words T H E S E and T H E I R?

d. What is an alternative to using the replace function to replace a single word?

35. Search and Replace

a. Describe the search and replace function in your own words.

b. What is meant by *global search and replace*?

c. What is meant by *the size of the replace area*?

d. List three things that can be specified in a search and replace menu.

36. Sort

a. What is an *alphanumeric character string*?

b. What is the difference between ascending and descending order?

c. Describe the difference between a *single-variable* and a *multiple-variable* sort.

d. In an ascending multiple-variable sort, which line of text would appear first in the following list?

	Column 1	*Column 2*
a.	Apples	1097
b.	Apricots	345
c.	Apples	1005

37. Repaginate

a. How does the repaginate function affect the number of lines per page?

b. How does changing margins affect the number of lines per page?

c. If the repaginate function is used to adjust page lengths to forty lines, how many pages will result from three 80-line pages?

d. How can the move function be used as a substitute for the repaginate function to adjust page lengths?

38. Block Protect

a. How is block-protected text affected when an entire document is reformatted?
b. How are the beginning and end points of the block to be protected typically identified?
c. What kinds of text are typically protected by the block protect function?
d. What can happen to a complex table if it is inadvertently reformatted?

39. Renumber

a. What is typically renumbered by the renumber function?
b. How is the renumber function used to accommodate switching pages or paragraphs within a document?
c. If page 1 is moved behind page 3 in a document, what will be the effect of the renumber function?
d. What is meant by an *extension number*? Give an example.

40. Hyphenation

a. How is the hyphenation function used in conjunction with the word wrap function?
b. How much text can typically be selected for hyphenation?
c. What is the *hyphenation zone*?
d. What is a word processing system hyphenation dictionary?

41. Spelling Dictionary

a. How many words are contained in a word processing system spelling dictionary?

b. What does the spelling dictionary function find when it is activated?

c. What can be done if a new, correctly spelled word is found by the spelling dictionary function?

d. How does the spelling dictionary save a word processing operator time?

42. *Automatic Table of Contents*

a. What information is created by the automatic table of contents function?

b. Define the term *front matter.*

c. How does the system find paragraph headings?

d. Where is the table of contents page normally found when filed in a document?

43. *List Merge*

a. Describe a *base document.*

b. What is meant by *list merge*?

c. What is an application of the list merge function?

d. Can variable information be merged in the body of a document?

44. *Document Assembly*

a. Describe the term *document assembly.*

b. What is an *object document*?

c. What is meant by *super copy*?

d. How can document assembly be used to create a legal document?

45. *Headers and Footers*

a. Define *headers* and *footers.*

b. What kind of information does a header typically include?

c. What kind of information does a footer typically include?

d. Where are odd and even page numbers normally positioned on a page?

46. *Automatic Right-Hand Justification*

a. Define *right-hand justification.*

b. What is the alternative to a right-hand justified margin?

c. What is the difference between character space and incremental space insertion, and which is preferred?

d. On systems that do not display justified text on the screen, where can justified text be verified?

47. *Printing*

a. Define *concurrent printing.*

b. How many characters per inch are printed using 12-pitch?

c. How many lines of text can be printed in three inches?

d. Define *proportional space type.*

48. *Printer Stop Code*

a. Describe the function of a printer stop code.

b. Are printer stop codes visible on the screen? Are they printed?

c. Describe how the stop code is used to type a word in italics.

d. How can the stop code be used to type a form having nonstandard line spacing?

49. Automatic Underscore and Deunderscore

a. Describe the difference between *underscore* and *deunderscore.*

b. What other term is sometimes used for *automatic underscore*?

c. In what two typical ways can underlines be entered beneath text?

d. Some systems cannot display an underscore beneath a character on the display screen. How can the area to be printed with underscores be defined?

50. Double Underscore

a. How are the beginning and end points of the text to be double underscored typically defined?

b. What is a popular use of the double underscore function?

51. Bold Print (or Shadow Print)

a. How is text made bolder by the word processing system printer?

b. How is the text to be printed bold typically identified?

c. What is an application of bold printing?

52. Subscript and Superscript

a. What is the difference between a *subscript* and a *superscript*?

b. Define the term *text baseline.*

c. How far above or below the baseline are subscripts and superscripts normally printed?

d. What are a few typical applications of subscripts and superscripts?

53. Overprint

a. How many characters are typically printed on the same spot by using the overprint function?
b. What does the printer do in response to the overprint function?
c. Describe how a zero and a slash sign can be combined using the overprint function.
d. Describe two applications of the overprint function.

54. Strike Through

a. Describe the strike through function in your own words.
b. How are the beginning and end points of text to be struck through identified?
c. What is meant by an *imbedded code*?
d. What is an application of the strike through function?

55. No Print

a. What is accomplished by the no print function?
b. How is the text to be no printed defined?
c. Describe an application of the no print function.

56. Printing Special Characters and Symbols

a. What is meant by *special characters*?
b. How are reference books and cards used to find special characters?
c. What is an advantage of having a dual-head printer?
d. What is meant by *supershift*?

57. *Reverse Roll (or Top of Form)*

a. Describe what happens to the page being printed when the reverse roll function is used.

b. How does the printer detect when it is time to perform a reverse roll?

c. Describe how the reverse roll function is used to type two-column text on a single sheet of paper.

d. Describe how the reverse roll function is used to type a document using two type styles.

58. *Type Through (or Typewriter Mode)*

a. What is an advantage of the type through function?

b. When in the type through mode, what happens when the word processing system operator types on the keyboard?

c. Name some typical uses of the type through mode.

59. *Glossary (or User Defined Keys)*

a. Describe how the glossary function saves a word processing operator time.

b. What is meant by a *glossary keystroke label*?

c. When a glossary key sequence is recalled, what happens on the display screen?

60. *Mathematical Function*

a. What is another term for the *mathematical function*?

b. What four mathematical operators are typically used by the mathematical function?

c. Describe what is meant by the expression

$$R3C2 = R1C2 + R2C2$$

d. What is meant by a number in parentheses?

61. Telecommunications

a. List five important elements required for telecommunications.

b. What is a *communications menu*?

c. What is the purpose of telephone interface equipment?

d. What is another term for *telecommunications*?

INDEX